BIKING THROUGH

It's About Time

by Paul V. Stutzman

Dedicated to Ivan J. Schlabach
November 15, 1951–September 5, 1966
He was the first person I knew to truly go home.

We thought we had all the time in the world...

TABLE OF CONTENTS

Table of Contents

CHAPTER 1

The Roadmaster

The old green bicycle would rattle around the last curve in the road, and I'd catch sight of our house. I could feel the warmth of home spreading through my spirit much like the summer sun soaked my skinny young body.

Whether I was voyaging down gravel roads on that old bike or roaming the woods, damming creeks and capturing minnows with my mason jar, I made certain that as evening came on I was close enough to the house to hear Mom's cry from the porch, "It's suppertime!" When my four sisters chimed in, the call to come home reverberated over hill and valley.

The woods were my escape when I felt I had too many sisters. They all had a brother, but I did not; and being the only boy, I became adept at finding adventure on my own. The woods bordered open fields on both the north and south sides of our house at the edge of Benton, and I'd ramble alone for hours. Today parents would panic and report children missing if they disappeared for as much of the day as I did when I was a boy.

My parents didn't always know where I roamed, but I had self-defined limits in those woods and seldom crossed my own boundaries. Every now and then, curiosity did get the better of me and

I'd step out to explore new territory, only to quickly return to my realm of safety. It felt good to know home was nearby.

We were happy, even though we never really stopped to think about it. We had so little, and we were content. It took the passage of many years and much living for us to appreciate how idyllic life was at our home back in the fifties.

No matter where I roamed in my youthful adventures, I looked forward to coming home to Mom and Dad and my four sisters at day's end. I knew we'd soon be gathering at the supper table, eating and laughing together.

Suppertime was a major two-prayer event at our house. Since there was no radio or television to divert our attention, meeting at the supper table was the focal point of our day. We each had assigned seats around the table. I had a prized chair by the picture window until I was caught using the curtain as a napkin and thus lost that spot. No one left the table until the plates were cleared and that second prayer was said.

I was a particularly finicky eater, and at times this caused much consternation at the supper table. On one occasion, I was convinced a small bug had landed in my bowl of noodles and I refused to eat them. I was not permitted to leave the table until I had eaten my food; so when the rest of the family departed to visit Grandmother, they left me alone at the table with my plate of cold noodles. When they returned hours later, one stubborn boy was still sitting there with an uneaten bowl of noodles before him. My father then became a believer, accepted the probability that a bug was indeed an ingredient in my supper, and excused me from the table.

Long before my family returned, I myself had realized that the "bug" was probably just a speck of parsley, but I was too far down the road of stubbornness to give up at that point. Although it was a foolish waste of time and noodles, that incident gave a glimpse of the tenacity that would carry me through periods of doubt and discouragement on my future hiking and biking trips.

Second only to time spent together as a family was time spent in church. Our family had left the Amish faith for a Conservative

Mennonite congregation, where new edicts on life and conduct loaded heavy burdens of guilt on my young conscience.

Words from the pulpit warned of the evils of reading comic strips and fairy tales. With no radio or television, I dove into reading as another favorite escape. From the moment I could read, I saw the daily newspaper as my lifeline to another world. I read everything, but I most anticipated following the daily adventures of the detective Dick Tracy. And I just had to know what Skeezix was up to in "Gasoline Alley." But suddenly, watching Dagwood trying to stay in the good graces of Blondie became a sin. How could the adventures of eight-year-old Nancy and her friend Sluggo be so detrimental to my spiritual well-being? I read "Joe Palooka," the strip about the heavyweight boxer, with much guilt. A trip to the library created more consternation when I checked out a book called *Grimm's Fairy Tales*.

My reading now required more time; after every comic strip and every page in my book of fairy tales, I would pause and beg God's forgiveness for my wickedness. Grace was an entity unknown to a young boy carrying so much guilt. This was the tightrope I walked, wanting to do what was right but knowing that almost everything I did was wrong. According to the preachers, Jesus was returning to the earth at any minute; and I just knew He would come while I was reading the comic strips and I'd be left behind.

One advantage of our move to a Mennonite church was that we could trade our horse and buggy for a Studebaker; we now traveled greater distances with ease. I didn't know much about cars, but I did know this car was ugly. The floorboards were rusted and one rear door sometimes flew open unexpectedly. The Studebaker had no turn signals, so Dad would stick his arm out the window to indicate which way he was turning. I often sat on his lap and took on the task of showing the driver behind us what turn to expect. My skinny arm darted out, pointing upward for a right turn and downward for a left.

At least once a week our family would pile into that old Studebaker for a trip to Grandma's farm at the edge of a neighboring town, and what made the trip to Grandmother's house extra special was what awaited me there—happiness on two wheels, a bicycle.

As a younger boy, I did not have a bicycle. My friends all had bikes, but we could not afford to buy one. I begged and pleaded to no avail. Money was needed for food and clothing, not for a two-wheeled contraption that took so much work to operate. I often dreamed about the freedom of the open road, but oh! if only I had a bicycle. At my grandmother's house, one much-used bicycle gave me a taste of my dream.

To my surprise, there was more to riding a bike than simply jumping on and pedaling away. My first ride down Grandmother's lawn was disastrous. I ate more grass than most grazing animals that day. But finally I wobbled out onto the road. The moment was magic. I was actually moving, at least for a short distance. Then… Ouch! The grass had tasted better than the road. In spite of several more tumbles, I was hooked. Soon I pedaled all the way to the neighbor's house and back without mishap.

The begging and pleading intensified. "Dad, I just have to have a bicycle. I'll do anything. I'll work extra in the garden, I'll quit reading the comics, and I'll behave real good." I made every promise I could think of.

Then one day it happened. Dad had visited his older brother, who had a bicycle that no one used, and my uncle gave it to my dad. This bike was very much like the Studebaker; it was green, it was old, and it was ugly. The old Roadmaster rolled along on huge balloon tires and weighed close to fifty pounds. The leather covering on the seat had worn off at places, exposing the metal surface. What leather remained was split by a jagged crack that would, on occasion, send a piercing pain through my body when my seat moved the wrong way on the bike seat. But none of that mattered; I finally had a bike.

Perhaps "we had a bike" is more accurate, since my sisters took claim to it also. The following morning, we were out of bed early, racing to take the first ride. We set up a course that looped through the garage and around the front of the house. An order was established, and each sibling got ten laps on the course.

We also had assigned chores to finish before bike riding, and mine was to hoe several rows in our huge garden. I attacked those rows in a frenzy. Much to my father's dismay, many innocent little stalks were sacrificed as the hoe slashed through rows of sweet corn. While my sisters were still occupied with their own chores, I took to the highway for my first road trip.

I traveled a great distance from my home that day. I passed our neighbor's house, and still I kept going. The rhythm soon came. Pedal, push, pedal, push. Anything more than a gradual incline couldn't be pedaled on our single-speed tank. It was like hiking with a bike. But, oh!, such a feeling of freedom on that half-mile adventure!

Day after day, I kept pushing my rides to new boundaries. My uncle had a farm three miles away at Honey Run, and three times a week the old Roadmaster and I made that ride. West on State Route 241, then left at Benton Mart's shoe repair shop, where I turned down a small gravel road. Gravel was no problem for this bike; the balloon tires would make today's mountain bike tires blush. Push up one hill, then zoom down the other side. The huge fender stopped any dust, dirt, or moisture flying upward.

On my way down one particular hill, I'd bring the bike to a skidding halt. This was a routine stop, an opportunity to rummage through the nearby dump.

It's hard to imagine today, but back in the fifties and early sixties folks would dump their garbage at several locations along the gravel roads. I had discovered great treasures in this particular dump. Piles of comic books had been left there, and I sat amid heaps of rubbish and became acquainted with the Flintstones, Casper the friendly ghost, Archie and Veronica and Jughead, Mickey Mouse, and Daffy Duck. Then, in hopes of many future readings, I'd conceal my treasure pile and extricate myself from the junk heap. As I continued my ride, I'd also say my prayer begging forgiveness for reading such trash.

This was my routine for several glorious summers, but I feared it was just a matter of time until the preachers declared the bicycle to be sinful. I suspected that anything so enjoyable surely could not be edifying.

My friend Ivan lived several miles in the opposite direction, and one day he invited me to his house to see his new bike, an incredible, two-wheeled wonder called an English bike. This masterpiece had three gears, handlebars that looked like ram's horns, and skinny tires. The bike was very light and the brakes were operated from the handlebars. What a spectacular feat of modern engineering. In awe I mounted that showpiece of techno-logical movement and pedaled away.

"This thing has no brakes!" I yelled.

"Squeeze the handbrakes," Ivan yelled back. He also yelled something about not squeezing the one brake lever alone or you'd get thrown off. At least, that was the message he intended to give; but it arrived to my ears a little late and I was already flying off the seat toward the roadway. Those handlebars may have given the appearance of a ram, but in reality the marvelous English bike rode like a bucking bronco.

Between gasps of laughter, Ivan explained that using only the front brake actually lifted the back of the bike off the ground. Of course, I had already learned that.

My fourteenth birthday arrived and brought a marvelous gift. My father had somehow squeezed $40 out of the budget to buy me a bicycle, my very own shiny, red and white Schwinn. With three speeds and handbrakes, my new bike now carried me into the modern world. My explorations broadened and the limits of my comfort zone expanded.

Sadly, my idyllic world was about to be turned upside down. At far too young an age, I learned that life really is fragile. It's strange that in my memory of that tragic day, time seems to slow to a crawl. Conversations and events are forever etched in my memory.

Ivan was biking to my house that evening, and together we would ride to my cousin's house over at Honey Run for a sleepover.

I can still see Ivan pedaling up our driveway and engaging my dad in a conversation about gravel. His dad owned several dump trucks and hauled gravel and other aggregates for driveways and construction sites. Ivan suggested a certain grade of gravel my dad should purchase, and then we were off for the night.

We two were meandering up the road on our bikes when a young man from my church met us. He was several years older than I was and was driving his car. He stopped to ask what we were up to, we chatted a while, and he drove off.

When we're young, we think things will always be the same. We have our families, our friends are always part of our lives, and time moves slowly. After that evening, forty-four years would go by before I again saw that friend who stopped to chat. And that night would be the last time Ivan and I were together on this earth.

At eleven o'clock, we three were still full of youthful energy and decided to take a night bike ride. We headed out the long gravel driveway that led to the quiet country road. At the end of the drive, we stopped and chatted in the moonlight for several minutes. Then the question was which way to turn. The road to the right was level and an easier ride. Going to the left required a climb, but our reward would be an exhilarating downhill flight.

Most decisions we make in life are insignificant, or so we think. But sometimes a seemingly small choice can have unexpected consequences that change the course of a life. Ivan made the call that night. "Let's go left," he said. That decision cost him his life. What might have been different if we had gone right? What if we had stayed home that night, never got on our bikes?

We were flying back down the hill when tragedy struck. Ivan's bike veered onto the shoulder where the gravel grabbed the thin tires. My friend couldn't regain control. A bridge crossing a small stream loomed ahead of us. The bike hurtled down the creek bank and Ivan was launched across the stream, striking his head on a wooden retaining wall on the opposite side of the water.

Until they rebuilt the bridge years later, the indentation carved by Ivan's glasses was still visible on those boards, a painful reminder of the uncertainties of life.

My friend passed away several days after the accident. He was fourteen when he died. I was fifteen, and this brutal dose of reality made me question everything I had been taught about God. I parked my bicycle in the garage, determined never to ride it again. The bike now represented pain, and in just a few days I had enough of that to last a lifetime.

Seven months later I had my driver's license and the new freedom of driving a car. Who needs to ride a bicycle when you can drive a car? My mother sold the Schwinn at a garage sale; and for the next twenty-five years, the thought of getting back on a bicycle never entered my mind.

CHAPTER 2

Back to Biking

Those carefree childhood days spent exploring the woods and pedaling quiet country roads gave me no warning of how stressful life would become. Of course I could not have known; I was a child. But as I came into manhood and embarked on my quest to conquer the world while gaining an education, a wife and three children, plus car payments, house payments, and a job in the hospitality industry, the stress levels in my life skyrocketed.

Being in the hospitality business means, of course, that the job is all about dealing with the public. I might have guessed at the stress associated with that; what I was not prepared for was the toll taken by daily operations problems and employee issues.

I was a restaurant manager. That sounds like an easy job. A restaurant is a building, so I was managing a building. How hard can that be? Okay, so the building is full of employees, but how difficult can it be to manage employees? Okay, so my employees were mostly ladies...

How was it that growing up with four sisters and living hopelessly outnumbered by the female gender did not prepare me for managing a large number of women?

Lest I am misunderstood, before I go any further I will say that in twenty-five years of restaurant management I hired and worked with several thousand ladies and most were wonderful people. I am a firm believer in the equality of pay and opportunity for both sexes. It is a pleasure to watch the creativity of an employee doing what she enjoys, and I did have many strong and excellent employees. I was always happy to promote and give opportunities to those who were deserving.

But I also understand that when God created man and woman, he created different temperaments and perspectives. At the restaurant, my education began in this minefield, and I needed to adapt and learn—quickly.

I set out to fix everyone's problems. We men are fixers, but I learned that discerning what can't be fixed is essential. Keeping everyone happy is a hopeless and impossible task. Not all complaints have a solution; as a matter of fact, a solution is often not required or even desired. Listening and expressing concern is often more important than solving the problem. In a building full of actions, ideas, and emotions that were not always conducive to a productive work environment, I was the umpire.

And, as in any business, there were employees who were truly difficult, often possessing a strong personality that made them leaders of their peers. A deserving employee given a promotion will be loyal until death. An undeserving employee given a promotion will hasten that event.

Remember that I grew up in a farming community, a lifestyle that would seem far removed from the world of business and commerce. Yet I have seen many principles in business that have parallels in farming. And here I am referring to the pecking order of chickens and the phenomenon of the lead cow.

Most of you probably have read about the pecking order among chickens, an established ranking where the strongest bird rules the roost. Did you know there's always a "lead cow"? Other members of the herd take their cues from the lead cow. The interesting thing is that if you slaughter or otherwise remove the lead cow or the chicken that rules the roost, another leader always steps in and assumes the role.

What's the point of all this barnyard psychology? Human groups function in the same way, with the strongest person becoming a leader that gives direction and influences the rest of the group. Now, this is great news for a manager if that strong employee happens to be a positive influence among the workforce. But if the natural leader who has emerged has another agenda, if that person is constantly at odds with owners or managers, then the business and the manager's sanity both suffer.

What to do about such an employee? It's impossible to fire your way out of this predicament. Another leader—whether hurtful or helpful—steps up and fills the spot. There is only one solution; you must be intuitive, prudent, quick-witted, bold, and perceptive. Throw in a lot of common sense and prayer. A thick skin helps, too.

I learned many survival tips, but the daily stress of management took a toll and I needed a respite. I'd daydream about hiking in the woods and reminisce about those carefree days on my bicycle. Those boyhood bike rides had given me such a sense of freedom. I'd taken no interest in riding a bicycle for all of the twenty-five years since Ivan's accident. But now I was beginning to wonder— might a bike ride be a good antidote for a stressful day?

Amish Country in Holmes County, Ohio, was a quiet and insulated community during the fifties and sixties. Quaint, well-kept farms dotted the landscape and most of the Amish were farmers. As the Amish and Mennonite population grew, finding suitable occupations became more difficult. A migration of Amish families took place, with families moving to states such as Kentucky, Tennessee, and Missouri.

Even so, not enough farms were available to provide employment and livelihoods. The creativity and work ethic of the Amish community manifested itself as small shops began to sell crafts and furniture. As the world started to recognize the quality craftsmanship coming from our community, Amish Country became a travel destination.

The tourist industry discovered the quiet, peaceful community that we had all taken for granted. More tourists appeared; more shops opened. Soon restaurants, cheese houses, hotels, and furniture shops were sprouting up everywhere. Jobs were suddenly plentiful, and an increasing number of the Amish were no longer farming but "working away."

Transportation now became a problem. Many businesses provided drivers to bring their Amish employees to work, but smaller shops found this impossible. The most logical mode of transportation became the bicycle.

What had been such a novelty for me as a boy is the norm in my adult world. Today there are more bike shops in Amish Country than car dealerships. Bicycles are as much a part of everyday life for the Amish community as the horse and buggy. It is not unusual to see dozens of bicycles parked in a field where a volleyball game is in progress. How fortunate that ministers, while discerning right from wrong, didn't pronounce this two-wheeled mode of transportation too worldly.

After Ivan's accident, I had given up my bike adventures. I soon turned sixteen and traded two wheels in for four; Dad's 1959 Pontiac now expanded my horizons. Instead of pedaling several miles to a destination, I traveled to places my old Roadmaster could never reach. I didn't have to push the Pontiac up hills, and its seat never pinched me. Bicycling was the furthest thing from my mind.

But as an adult seeking escape from the stress of my life, I again went riding on two wheels. I bought a Schwinn bicycle from a co-worker for $100. The bike was several years old, but still an upgrade from my last three-speed Schwinn. My riding changed, too. On my boyhood rides, the destination was always the goal; now my goal was the ride itself.

My very first ride as an adult took me through the rural countryside and past familiar scenes. The aroma of wood smoke curling from a chimney brought back memories from many years ago. Well-tended flowerbeds and gardens reminded me of my childhood home. I heard a soft putt-putting sound from a gas-powered washing machine and I was a boy again, waking up at my grandmother's house on the farm on washday.

It's strange how the same sound can take on different qualities. Let me explain.

When I was a child, every night at eleven o'clock a train passed through a neighboring town five miles west of our house. I never actually saw this train, but it still was a part of my being. I would open my window and hear the rhythmic sound of metal wheels clicking over rails. As the train approached town, a lonely whistle drifted on the wind to my open window. Those predictable sounds in the night had been soothing to a young boy. On my Appalachian Trail hike in 2008, I often lay in my tent up in the mountains and listened to distant trains passing through Appalachian towns. The rhythmic sounds always took me back to my childhood home.

On that same hike, I spent a night in Duncannon, Pennsylvania. Outside my open fourth-floor window ran several railroad tracks. All night long trains blasted through town, and piercing whistles and annoying clacking of metal on metal kept me awake. That night, those sounds were just aggravating *noise* because I was too close to the situation.

When I was a teenager, a similar noisy encounter turned into a poignant moment of reflection. My best friend had just dropped me off at my home. The muffler on his car was gone, and our ride had been less than pleasant. As he roared away from my house, I recoiled at the blast of noise spewing from the car.

It was a calm, wind-free night and I was still outside gazing at stars in the vast universe, when I realized I could hear my friend's car in the distance. I heard him shift through the gears as he changed directions. The sound of the engine told me when he picked up speed or slowed down for curves and when he turned right at The Plains crossroads.

However, now I was listening to sounds, not the noise that had blasted me in my driveway. These sounds were pleasant as they slowly became softer with increasing distance. I stood outside and followed the sounds of my friend's car all the way to his house, miles away. Finally there was silence, followed by the sound of a car door slamming shut. On the gentle night air, those sounds drifted over the miles from my friend's house at Martins Creek, above hill and vale, over the small cemetery where my grandfather and other Amish relatives were buried, all the way to my home at the edge of Benton.

The annoying noise had turned to sounds that spoke of friendship and of a golden era of childhood coming to an end. For a few reflective moments as I stood under the stars, those sounds gave me a clear picture of my life. I was fortunate and I knew it. God had placed me in a Christian family with wonderful parents and great sisters; I had many friends and a church that really did care for me in spite of my tendency to push the limits. I had a vague sense of life awaiting me, manhood and marriage and career; but I had no idea of the happiness and heartaches ahead.

Life can be noisy. We can be so close to situations that we really can't discern what the din and clatter is all about. Distancing ourselves sometimes helps us understand and comprehend what is really happening to us.

That first bike ride through the familiar countryside gave me distance from up-close reality, took me to places of comfort and peace, and put my life in perspective. And so, in the din and clatter of the stress of my adult life, I went bike riding again.

CHAPTER 3

Decision Time

On a gorgeous Fourth of July in the summer of 2008, I walked the streets of Dalton, Massachusetts, lost in thought, contemplating the vagaries of life that had brought me to this place at this time. My friend Padre walked beside me. A Mennonite man and a Catholic priest. That picture alone was incredible, almost too strange to be true. I was hiking the Appalachian Trail after losing my wife; Padre the priest was on a sabbatical and fulfilling a lifetime dream. We were both intent on completing the 2,176-mile journey over 300 mountains and fourteen states.

As I walked, my mind drifted back to my previous life. So many changes had occurred in just a few years. My world had been turned upside down. Some folks relish a life that is in constant transformation. I suppose change is inevitable; but I embrace it reluctantly, preferring routine and stability. Sure, I enjoyed adventures, new trails to hike, and new bike routes to explore; but after every new adventure, I could return to my wife and family, and my home kept me centered. That had all changed. The children were grown and cancer had taken my wife from me.

When we are young, time seems to drag by slowly. We think the day will never come when we can be in charge of our own lives. When we are young, we just assume our needs will be met.

We have a home, we have food on the table, and we have parents who care for us. But the day finally arrives when we walk away from our childhood. This usually involves a walk down the aisle. We are in love; all is well. No more parents asking why we came home so late. No more curfews, no more school. Free at last. Time to conquer the world.

And then it happens. Life whacks us upside the head with reality. We become parents, and the joy attending the arrival of a new baby is tempered with the expense of raising a child. Marriage and a family assure that things never stay the same.

The day did arrive when the children were grown and my wife and I looked forward to enjoying new freedoms. The angel of death, however, did not consider our wishes when it arrived at our house that night in September 2006. At the time, it was difficult to imagine that God had a plan or even cared about the pain our family felt at losing mother and wife.

But on my hike in the wilderness, God gave me a new understanding of His grace and love. I marveled at the changes that took place in my soul. A serene peace settled into my being.

As we strolled through Dalton that day, we heard laughter from front porches and lawns. Padre and I spoke of our own homes and families. He had been raised on a farm in a large family; and in his youth, suppertime was an important event, just as it was in my home. I was struck by the significance of family. Family represented safety, acceptance, and being loved.

"Padre," I said, returning again to the present, "I believe this is a picture of what Heaven is like, with families playing and laughing together and everyone accepted and wanted."

A thought crept into my mind, a thought so bizarre that in my previous life it would have been immediately rejected because it was far beyond my comfort zone. But since my wife's death, that zone no longer existed; and somehow this idea made sense on that Fourth of July in 2008.

"When this hike is over," I told my friend, "I'm going to ride my bicycle across America. I want to visit with folks that I meet and hear their stories." There had to be more places like Dalton, where families were still honored. I wanted to find those places.

My bold statement ignored two facts: I had never biked more than sixty miles in one day, and as a young boy, I'd always felt uneasy riding more than several miles from home. But I had done the unthinkable and quit a good job to hike the Appalachian Trail. Now a cross-country bike trip made sense…almost.

On August 13, 2008, I summited Mt. Katahdin in Maine and completed my Appalachian Trail journey. The AT hike had brought healing to my soul and a contentment that had eluded me all my adult life. A new path lay ahead of me, a path filled with many unknowns. I had retired from a twenty-five-year restaurant career and had left for the trail immediately. Once the hike was finished, it took some time to form new habits and patterns of living. My routine eventually emerged, and my days were focused on writing a book. And, of course, I finally had time to ride my bicycle whenever I wished.

I now was the owner of two bicycles. For my explorations on the smaller dirt roads in Amish Country, I rode a hybrid bike with suspension and wider tires. My second bike was a bright red, carbon fiber racing bike with the latest gizmos and gadgets. This lightweight beauty of rapid motion had cost me almost as much as I had paid for my first car. With those ram-horn handlebars and a tiny seat perched high in the air, I was the ruler of the road. When I shoved my slightly overweight body into a pair of tight biker shorts, I could almost have passed for a real biker.

The racing bike would have been a joy, I suppose, for a person who likes to ride hunched over, watching the tarmac fly by. I, however, didn't enjoy that type of ride. I wanted to sit upright and see my surroundings. I wanted to watch the farmers as they plowed their fields. I enjoyed seeing those little green shoots of corn arising from the brown earth as I pedaled by. I sold the racer.

When I rediscovered the rewards of biking, I charted out numerous routes from my house in Berlin and gave each ride a name.

"Where are you going today?" Wifee would ask me as I rushed out of the house after another stressful day.

"Oh, the flower route," I would reply. That was a seven-mile loop with numerous gardens to enjoy. If I replied, "I'm going around the block," my wife knew I was headed out for a fifteen-mile ride that took me past my grandmother's farm. Going around the block was my favorite route; it held many pleasant memories from long ago.

In the second springtime after my AT hike, I was riding through Amish Country, around the block. The stretch of road where I had first learned to ride a bicycle was a short distance ahead.

Also ahead was a team of draft horses pulling a full manure wagon. The steel wheels clattered as the loaded wagon made its way to the field where the manure would be spread. *Oops! Look out. Watch where you're riding*, I reminded myself. I stopped to take in the scene. Cloudlets of vapor billowed from the heaving nostrils of the horses as they maneuvered the wagon across the field. I admired the flight of the steaming clods, rising from the spreader, arcing toward the sky, and then falling to the soil where they would add nutrients for the year's corn crop.

As I passed my grandmother's farm, I recounted good memories of all the times spent there. I regretted that a bowl of noodles had kept me from one visit. What did I miss that evening? What would Grandmother and I have talked about that night, had I not been so stubborn? Had fifty-some years already passed since I sat for hours in front of a little leaf of parsley in cold noodles?

As my life settled into a routine after my Appalachian Trail hike, I found myself frequently retreating into memories of the past rather than dreaming about boldly attacking life and making new memories. I was too often looking in the rearview mirror, rather than striking out on new paths. I knew I had settled into comfortable habits and I would be stuck in those patterns—unless I made a difficult choice.

While hiking the Appalachian Trail, I had determined to ride my bicycle across America. Almost two years after my hike, I admitted that I needed a new challenge; but I was comfortable in my routine of riding those short routes and always arriving back at the safety of my own home. Still, the idea of a bike ride across America had never left my mind.

We are given a lot of choices and pathways in life. I believe God wants the best for each of our lives, but He won't make the decisions for us. He will give guidance, but He waits for us to make our own choices. And sometimes, I imagine that He probably wishes we would just make up our minds and *do something* so that He can work and meet us on the path we've chosen.

I constantly debated with myself about the bike trip. I knew I needed to challenge myself, but I was too comfortable, too safe. I was fine with postponing the ride; I rather preferred staying home. By now, the thought of being alone on a bicycle thousands of miles from home did not hold the same allure that it had on the day I walked through Dalton with Padre. I wavered and could not solidify plans to start the ride. Recalling how clearly God had revealed to me that the time was right to leave my employment and hike the Appalachian Trail, I wondered if His direction would come to me again with such clarity.

The answer did come. I had given myself a deadline; the decision must be made by a certain date if I was to have enough time to buy equipment and do the planning necessary to bike from one end of America to the other. The morning of my self-imposed deadline arrived, and I had no clear answer to my dilemma. I fell to my knees and asked God for some guidance in this difficult choice.

Finished with my appeals to God, I walked uptown to the post office. Once again, I was reminded that God does work in mysterious ways. In the few minutes I was in the post office, five people asked me when I would be starting my cross-country bike ride.

"I believe it will be this summer," I told messenger number five. A feeling of relief filled me. The decision had been made.

How do I get across America on a bicycle? So many roads criss-cross this country, how does one choose which routes to take? What bicycle do I ride? Should I buy a new one? Where do I stay? What equipment do I need? I recalled the uncertainties of my hiking trip and how I had been assisted by a knowledgeable salesman at the outfitting store. I needed a biking expert.

A new bike shop had opened in my parents' neighborhood, just up the road from their house. The shop was located along my childhood bike route to my cousin's house and my old landfill library. It seemed appropriate to start there.

The new salesroom had a huge selection of bikes in many different brands. I explained my plan to the owner and asked which bike he would choose if he'd be doing such a trip. He showed me a white, thirty-speed bike with an aluminum frame and carbon fiber forks. "This Specialized Sirrus will get the job done," he promised.

The deal was done; and after purchasing lights, a tool kit, panniers, and extra tubes, I was outfitted.

"Just one more thing. I need to measure you," said the owner. Measure me? Am I buying a new suit? No, he informed me he would measure my legs to adjust the proper height and angle of the seat. I wondered if the seat would be comfortable for such a long ride. He assured me I was buying the best seat available.

The only decision remaining was where to start and where to finish this bike adventure. (Oh, yes, and I probably should inform the kids about my next foray into the unknown.) I knew that the mileage on a cross-country trip was about 3,000 miles. I also was aware that each year many riders completed the journey. *Far too many,* I thought, wondering if maybe this was a sign that the ride would be *too* easy.

I had a logical solution. With the aid of the Internet and the power granted to me by Google, I set about finding my starting and finishing points. My idea was to find the farthest two points in America and make the trip from one to the other. I also knew I wanted to travel from west to east, hopefully having the advantage of winds at my back.

I was familiar with the southernmost corner of America. My wife and I had visited Key West, Florida, years before and I relished a return trip there. The northwestern corner was a town I had never heard of, Neah Bay, on the far corner of the Olympic peninsula in the state of Washington. Several miles west of this town, a three-quarter-mile trail leads through wetlands and cedar trees to the geographical northwestern corner of the contiguous United States, a dramatic overlook on the cliffs facing the Pacific Ocean.

I'd take a flight to Seattle, but I had no idea how my bike and I would get to Neah Bay, yet another 160 miles northwest of Seattle. Bob Hackney, a retired friend of a friend, lived in the Seattle area; and when he learned of my plans, he offered to pick me up at the airport and transport myself and my bicycle to my starting point. Bob found a bicycle shop convenient to our intended route, and I packed up my new bike and shipped it there to await my arrival.

No more casual little rides around the block. It was time to go biking across America.

CHAPTER 4

Only 5,000 More Miles

I had often thought that if I ever walked off an airplane and was met by someone holding a placard bearing my name, then I would have "arrived" in more ways than just one. My social status must have been elevated sometime during the flight between Ohio and Washington; when I stepped off the plane in Seattle, a stranger stood there in the crowd, holding a sign with my name on it. The newly acquired status, however, felt no different from my lowly existence prior to the flight.

Behind the placard was Bob Hackney. We had never met, but his assistance as my contact in the Pacific Northwest was extremely helpful. He had learned about my trip and thought it would be exciting to be involved in the launch of my adventure. Retired, Bob was an avid fisherman and had fished off the coast of Neah Bay.

After exchanging greetings, we headed north to pick up my bike at a bicycle shop in Lynnwood. Bob had even visited the shop previously to make sure UPS had done its job and the bike had arrived. As we drove, he pointed out places of local interest, but we could not dawdle at sightseeing.

"We need to catch the ferry to cross Puget Sound," he reminded me. Puget Sound is the body of water separating the Olympic Peninsula from the mainland. I had assumed a bridge crossed the sound, and my limited planning had not considered that I might, instead, have to schedule a ferry crossing. By the time we had made the six-mile crossing from Edmonds to Kingston, it was too late to drive the entire distance to Neah Bay.

We stopped in the little fishing village of Sequim, in an area called the Lavender Capital of North America. With a climate perfect for the plant, many farms there grow lavender commercially. It was the height of the season, and we passed fields with mounded rows of flowers in full bloom.

The next morning we drove Route 112, a hilly and winding road that follows the coast and gives splendid views over the ocean. Canada and Vancouver Island were visible off to our right, across the water.

Nearing our destination, we were greeted by a sign that read, WELCOME TO THE MAKAH NATION. Neah Bay is located on an Indian reservation. Whether by design or by chance, native Americans still control the northwest corner of the contiguous United States.

Another five miles beyond the town of Neah Bay is the Cape Trail. This path, maintained by the Makah tribe, leads through the cedar forest to Cape Flattery, my starting point. In some places, the trail is a pleasant stroll down a woodland path; other areas are damp and swampy, bridged by boardwalks. Not too strenuous a hike, it is nevertheless not a level walk; there were climbs and descents.

Although I enjoy tackling and conquering things that are difficult, I don't aspire to be the first person to do anything. I do believe, however, that I was the first to ever push, pull, lift, and carry a bicycle to the lookout point at the end of the Cape Trail. The trail was meant for walkers, not riders. I walked the bike along bumpy and narrow boardwalks, carried it up and down wooden steps, and lifted it over rocks and roots. The bike had to be with me at that starting point on the cape; it just didn't seem right to begin a cross-country bicycle trip without the bicycle.

Reaching the terminus of the trail, we were met by stunning views as we stood on the observation platform high above the ocean. Huge rock formations stood offshore, sculpted into odd shapes by the powerful sea; dark indentations in the cliffs were sea caves that had been pounded out by incessant waves. This was my first glimpse of the dramatic views that awaited me all along the northwestern coastline.

Bob and I both snapped photos. It was a beautiful place, but my mind was on the reason I had come. I backed my bicycle up to the very edge of a sheer cliff, the very edge of America, and Bob's camera documented the start of my journey. The time had come to depart for Key West, Florida, the opposite corner of our country, only 5,000 miles away.

Back at the small parking area, I strapped on the bike panniers, Bob took a few more pictures, and I started pedaling.

The day was Saturday, July 10.

The beginning of any adventure such as this holds so many uncertainties. On those first five miles downhill returning to Neah Bay, at the edge of the Olympic Mountain range, I coasted along in quiet contemplation. Mist from the Pacific Ocean drifted down and soaked me as my mind wandered back over the past ten years.

I was no longer on the well-planned pathway I had laid out for myself. My goal had been to get out of debt and store up some financial resources. Then, at a future date, my wife and I could volunteer time to do mission work. But the death of my spouse had caused me to rethink all my previous priorities. After Mary was gone, storing up resources for some uncertain future no longer seemed a compelling goal. A previously unthinkable move began to seem logical: I would quit my job and follow a different pathway. I would leave my comfort zone and trust that God would lead me forward.

Here at the northwestern tip of America, I had certainly pushed far from my comfort zone. I was no longer able to round the bend of the road at day's end and see my home. I had no idea where this day's end would even find me.

A fan of moisture spraying from my tires buffeted my face and brought me back to the present. I rounded a bend and was back in the Makah Nation. I've always enjoyed studying maps and imagining how towns or road intersections look in reality. Once seen, though, many places lose that mystique of the unknown. This first town in my journey would have been better off left as a mystery. The reality of Neah Bay that I rode through was littered with ramshackle houses and mobile homes.

Leaving the town, I followed Route 112 for several miles until it intersected with Route 113, where I headed south. A short while later I was faced with a choice. Highway 101 circles the perimeter of the Olympic Peninsula. A left turn would take me east, back through Port Angeles along the same road Bob and I had traveled that morning to Neah Bay. A right turn would lead west and south through the town of Forks and on to the Pacific Coast. Both directions would eventually take me out of Washington and into Oregon. Just as in life, my choice of direction determined so many things. I wonder who I might have met, what I might have seen on the road not chosen. I decided to take the unknown road that led to Forks, Washington.

A tumult of emotions fueled my pedaling. The exhilaration of beginning a new adventure was tinged with uncertainty and apprehension. I like routine and dependability; but as I looked ahead, I saw only 5,000 miles of unknowns.

The rhythm and exertion of pedaling had a calming effect. Along the roadside, wild hollyhock bloomed in profusion. I started to take in my surroundings. The land was mountainous and heavily forested except for numerous areas populated only by large stumps. Here, clear cutting had taken place many years before and some growth was reappearing. I saw one enormous stump that had been cut decades ago. Then another tree had apparently grown from the top of the stump, and that second tree had recently also been harvested.

My first big hill required some effort; but as I'd learned long ago, big climbs offer the reward of a thrilling ride down the other side. That thrill never materialized. Instead, I was introduced to my first headwind. This was new; pedaling on the downside of a hill was something my old Roadmaster had never required me to do.

I also quickly realized how much road conditions were going to determine my speed and distance. The smooth asphalt turned to a coarser stone mixture and immediately knocked five miles per hour off my speed.

In a few short hours, I'd already learned important lessons about long-distance biking. Too much weight would slow me down. Road conditions and wind direction would determine how far I could travel. And one more problem had surfaced. My bike seat had become so uncomfortable that I thought it almost unbearable.

At five o'clock that evening I reached the town of Forks, Washington. My plan had been to travel several hours more and find a camping spot, but I realized I would need more luxury than my tent would afford. The camping area was another twenty miles down the road, and I really needed a shower and a good night's sleep.

There was not much choice of lodging. Searching for a vacancy, I heard that over forty rooms in town were taken by Coast Guard people. A few days before, a Coast Guard helicopter had crashed just off the coast of the Olympic Peninsula and three of the four people aboard had died. That had brought more Coast Guard personnel and the media to town. Added to that influx was an invasion by the Twilight people.

In the past, Forks was a sleepy logging town that most folks just passed through on the way to somewhere else. That had changed recently with a series of vampire books by author Stephanie Meyer. Her four books, called the Twilight series, were romance stories about vampires. Although the author had never been to Forks, she used a fictionalized version of that town as a setting for her novels. The town grasped this new attention, took advantage of the opportunities, and pretended that the vampire stories had really taken place there.

I found the town gripped by Twilight mania. Houses were designated as sites where events in the novels had taken place. An old pickup truck had been painted red and was masquerading as the vehicle used in the books. Of course everything was bogus, and the old saying about a sucker being born every minute was extravagantly exploited here—except that the suckers were coming into town in droves and so was the money. Twilight events were held all over town. Twilight specials were on the menu in restaurants. Stores offered Twilight gifts and paraphernalia.

Into this mix of nonsense and madness pedaled one tired and aching biker. My only goal was to find a cheap room, soak my weary bones, and get some rest. The marquees on the motels in town all proclaimed no vacancies. One sympathetic desk clerk made some calls and told me that the Dew Drop Inn still had a room.

I rode to the far end of town where the inn, a recently constructed motel, sat across the street from a hardware and grocery store where the main character in the Twilight books had supposedly worked. I was in luck. The room rate for this inn was advertised as $69. That was $69 more than I had intended to pay at the beginning of the day, but that was fifty-nine miles and many sore body parts ago.

"We have one room left," said the young man at the front desk. "It's a suite, and it will be $200."

I gasped and looked at him in shock.

"I don't want to buy your place; I just want to rent a room," I replied.

"It's the Bella suite, named after the main character in the Twilight series," hc replied. "The author herself slept in that room." Thus began my education about all things Twilight.

Since it was approaching twilight in my own day, I started negotiations with my adversary.

"I have called other inns, and this one suite is really the only room left in the entire town," he assured me.

I assured him that no one in his right mind would pay $200 for a room in Forks. By now I was tired and dejected and just wanted the comforts of a hot soak in a tub and a warm bed.

"How about $150?" I offered.

"I really shouldn't, and my boss will be unhappy if he finds out I let it go so cheap. But I suppose you can have it for that."

The deal was done, and I wheeled my bicycle down the hallway in anticipation of this spectacular suite.

The Bella suite was designated as such by a piece of paper taped to the outside of the door. I opened the door and stepped into my extravagant luxury. Even through my exhaustion I saw the obvious—a $69 room had been turned into a $200 suite. A tray with a bottle of grape juice and several pieces of chocolate candy greeted me. As much as $1.00 might have been spent on red and black ribbons draped around the room. The look was topped off by red and black sheets and blankets and thirteen pillows—I only needed one. Oh, well, the soak in the tub was worth almost $100.

I decided to cross the street and look for much-needed nourishment at the store where Bella once worked. As I was leaving the motel, the front desk clerk rounded a corner and headed up toward the second floor. He gave me a sheepish grin. He was carrying a tray with chocolate pieces and a bottle of juice that looked similar to the tray in my room. *Something about that silly grin doesn't quite make sense*, I thought to myself.

On my return from Bella's place of employment, I investigated what I already suspected. The scoundrel did have $69 rooms left but was turning them into $200 suites. Two more rooms had just been appointed as suites and marked as such by several new sheets of paper stuck to the doors. If folks called for rooms, he would have one room left; and when the suckers bit, a room would quickly be transformed into a suite.

I resisted the urge to go to the front desk and dispense some Mennonite justice. I sort of admired the rascal's business acumen. I comforted myself with the belief that someday the Dew Drop Inn would become an all-suite inn with many rooms featuring characters from my own books. Imagine the money this fellow could command for a room where both the author of the Twilight series and the author of this book had slept.

The following morning I was rested and ready for a full day of riding. At the edge of Forks stood a road sign telling me it was

105 miles to Aberdeen, Washington. *Wow*, I thought to myself, *that's a century. Can I pull that off?* A biker who does a "century" rides 100 miles in one day. I had always dreamed of riding a 100-mile day but had never succeeded. Well, okay, I'd never even attempted it before.

Let's go for it, a corner of my brain said. *Are you crazy?* my body replied. *This is only the second day of a long journey; let's use some common sense.*

But the sane part of me was overruled. It was a beautiful Sunday and the miles flew by, miles of forest, wildflowers, and sheer beauty. There were occasional sections of clear cutting where posted signs indicated when each section had been cut and when it was due to be harvested again. Sometimes the forest broke to give me views out over the hilly terrain. The road had its ups and downs, but nothing so steep that required enormous exertion.

Enveloped in morning mist, I reached the coast at a stretch of beach where the Pacific Ocean had washed thousands of logs ashore. The wind remained favorable and the temperature perfect for my longest ride ever. I reached the seventy-mile mark in relatively good shape; at mile eighty, I was gasping and wheezing and 100 miles looked impossible. *Only twenty-five more miles. You can do it*, said my brain to my body. It became an endurance contest, a test to see if my stubbornness and persistence could keep my body going long after it wanted to quit.

At five o'clock I reached the 100-mile mark. No town was in sight. I was totally alone, but I slammed on the brakes and celebrated my first century with a loud "Yippee!" Then I quickly finished the ride into Aberdeen. On only my second day out, I had already met one goal.

My goal the following day would be to reach the town of Astoria, Oregon, eighty-two miles south.

The air was filled with a damp cold as I meandered three miles through the streets of Aberdeen the next morning. I had learned how fast that cold Pacific mist could soak my clothes, so I wore my GORE-TEX rain top. I was dry, but not warm. Three hours of pedaling brought me to the town of Raymond, where a corner café named Corner Café enticed me in from the cold for a bowl of hot soup. I frittered away an hour while observing the comings and goings of a small town eatery.

Pedaling through the town of South Bend, I observed a large conveyor protruding from a building. What appeared to be oyster shells were carried up the conveyor and dropped into the back of a truck. I pulled off the road and watched the scene for a while. Traveling along the coast, I'd seen numerous fishing vessels putting out into the bay. I guessed this building played some part in oyster harvesting, but I had no idea what process was taking place inside.

Several miles later, curiosity got the best of me. I stopped at Goose Point Oysters along Willapa Bay and asked if they would allow me to tour their oyster processing plant. They were very accommodating, outfitted me with a hairnet, and invited me in. Inside, fifteen Hispanic workers were hard at work shucking and sorting the disgusting critters.

They offered me a raw oyster, white, slimy, gelatinous. Although I had never had the courage to eat one before, I decided to give it a try. I realize some folks think raw oysters are a delicacy; but in my case, it was not to be. I gagged. I knew I'd either have to lose the oyster now or risk losing both the oyster and my Corner Café soup. I barged out the door and heaved that badly damaged oyster back into the bay.

While waiting for my throat to stop constricting, I noticed thousands of pounds of shells, bagged and stacked nearby. I introduced myself to Hector and questioned him about the process of raising oysters. It certainly was not what I expected or could have imagined.

A nearby hatchery supplies oyster farmers with millions of larvae. These microscopic larvae are put into tanks of warm water and left to squirm about for several days. Previously inhabited oyster shells are then put into cages and lowered into the tanks. The larvae (called "spat") attach themselves to the shucked oyster shells, and the water temperature is gradually lowered to equal the temperature in the waters of the bay.

The huge cages are then loaded onto the oyster barge and dropped into the bay. After several months, the boat goes back out to bring up the cages filled with shells and the attached baby oysters. Cages are emptied and the oysters dumped on the barge. These "seed oysters" are then taken farther out into the bay and shoveled off the boat, scattered in an area that is alternately bay and mud flats, changing as the tide comes and goes. They are left here to mature for several years.

Oysters filter nutrients from the waters of the incoming tide that fill the bay; when the tide goes out, the shellfish are exposed on the muddy flats. The tides completely change the bay, and everything that happens must be scheduled to coincide with those changes. High and low tides occur at different times each day and are affected by the phase of the moon. Harvesting of the mature oysters must be scheduled taking all of this into consideration. Hector showed me his lunar calendar, used to predict the tides and plan the harvesting work.

Hector was preparing to head out to raise the large metal cages containing seed oysters, dump them on the barge, and distribute them evenly to grow for three more years. "Do you want to go out with us?" he asked.

I vacillated for a while. Hector said they'd be out on the bay for three hours. It was already two o'clock and Astoria was still four hours away. On the other hand, this trip was about meeting people and seeing new things. This opportunity definitely qualified on both counts.

As Hector and his three co-workers and I putt-putted out into the bay, he explained the entire oyster operation to me. It was really just a farm out at sea. They leased 600 acres, which was their oyster farm. Other farmers leased surrounding waters. Instead of fences marking boundaries, tree branches stuck in the muddy bottom designated territories. Hector had started years before, shucking oysters himself, and had worked his way up to captain of his own boat. I inquired about compensation for the men I'd seen furiously shucking. They are paid on incentive, paid by the pound. A good oyster shucker could make about $30 an hour.

In three hours, I learned more about oysters than I ever expected. It was now five o'clock and I was still forty miles from my destination of Astoria. I explained to Hector that I had wanted to be in Astoria by nightfall, and he offered a shorter route than the one I had planned.

"Where Route 101 turns right, you turn left onto Highway 4. Then take 401 south to the bridge." The bridge Hector was referring to was the Astoria-Megler Bridge. This four-mile bridge crosses the Columbia River at Point Ellice near Megler, Washington.

I took the route suggested by Hector, and as darkness approached I could see the lights of the bridge in the distance. Headed downhill, I heard a clatter that sounded as if something had fallen from the bike; but I couldn't detect what I might have lost.

As I entered the narrow two-lane bridge, I remembered something I'd read about this span over the Columbia. This bridge has almost no shoulder and is quite frightening. Pedestrians are not permitted to walk across the bridge. Bicyclists, however, are welcome to cross. *How strange*, I had thought at the time. *If you wanted to walk across, all you needed to do was purchase a dilapidated bike and push it.*

It was close to nine o'clock. Time to turn on that expensive light I had purchased and installed on the bike. I now realized what that clattering noise had been several miles back. The light was missing. By then, I was halfway across that frightening bridge without a headlight. Fortunately, my rear light worked.

I hugged the right barrier and slowly worked my way across the bridge. The traffic was not heavy; and whenever a car approached, I'd dismount and squeeze myself and my bike tightly against the barrier. The last mile of the crossing was an uphill pedal, climbing the arch of the bridge that allowed huge ships to pass below.

Somewhere on the bridge, as I rode nervously through the darkness, I left the state of Washington. The town of Astoria, Oregon, welcomed me at the other end of the span.

Astoria is a starting point for many cross-country bikers riding across the northern tier of America. On a directional sign just off the bridge, one arrow pointed left and one arrow pointed right. To the left was US Route 30 East. Had I turned in that direction, Route 30 would have taken me through Wooster, Ohio, and on to Atlantic City, New Jersey, cutting my route by almost 2,000 miles. Instead, I turned right onto Route 101. As with so many choices on my journey, Route 30 became the road not taken.

Shortly after nine o'clock, I checked into a motel in Astoria, hungry and exhausted. I was too tired and it was too late to go out for an oyster dinner. The young lady at the front desk took pity on me. While I unpacked my bike, she rummaged through the kitchen and fixed me a plate of breakfast food. I was grateful for such a kind deed. It was just the first of many kindnesses shown a solitary rider as he biked across America.

CHAPTER 5

Routines and Roadside Hardware

We humans seek routine. Routine holds comfort and safety, and disruptions that throw our routines completely off course can be quite unsettling and even painful.

You say you don't have routines? Or you claim that routine is not important to you? Do you always take one route, even though several routes are available? Do your mornings follow the same schedule, day after day? Is there a favorite shirt or dress you often wear? Or what about that chair that is *yours* to watch television or read the newspaper? Is there a favorite blanket that always must lie on your bed? Do you sit in the same place in church every Sunday?

Why do we follow such patterns? We settle into routine because it feels safe. Yes, even those of you who think routine is not important resort to habitual behavior. We all like the safety of known routines.

My life had been in a state of constant disruption lately. For over thirty years, my routine had consisted of going to work and then returning to the comforts of a home and family. Going home after a day of work or play soothed my soul. Going home is all about being safe, wanted, and needed.

I pedaled down the Pacific coastline, headed straight into the unknown. I had no idea what lay ahead of me. My routines of three decades were gone; in the two years since my return from the Appalachian Trail hike, I had begun to chisel out a new shape for my life, adopting new habits and daily rituals. Now it would be months before I could go home to the solace of that relatively new life. I needed to establish some routines on the road, something that added a small bit of predictability and consolation to my days. This was important in finding peace on my new journey.

And so I got up every day and went to work. My work now was pedaling my bicycle. The assignment for the day might be to reach some town seventy or eighty miles closer to Key West. Rather than the profit and loss statements that had measured my previous life, maps and miles traveled were the gauge of each day's efforts. (Yes, I take pleasure from the small successes of daily life.)

Coming home each night was now simply finding a room for my weary body and my bike. The bike stayed with me; all my worldly possessions were in the panniers. Instead of being greeted by spouse and family after a day of work, my reward now was a long soak in a hot bath. That soak became the incentive to reach my daily goal. Many times my weary body fell asleep in the tub and I'd awaken much later, looking every bit like a wrinkled newborn. Next came a search for food. And later, I would take out computer and maps to research and plan the following day's journey. My final act would be to send off my daily blog and my personal journal.

Once sequestered in my motel room, I'd settle into that evening routine and I was home. Yes, I had a different home every night; but each night, four walls and a roof represented safety at the end of another long day. And isn't that what routines are all about—feeling safe?

I settled quickly into my biking routine, a routine I hoped would bring me comfort and keep me one step ahead of loneliness and despair.

Leaving Astoria, I crossed two more bridges to take Lewis and Clark Road that would lead me to the coast and a day filled with spectacular scenery. Morning mist blew in from the ocean as I pedaled through the coastal towns of Seaside and Cannon Beach.

The dark mouth of a tunnel loomed ahead of me. As I neared it, I saw huge signs installed on either side of the entrance. Bikers wishing to enter the tunnel pushed a button to activate flashing lights on the signs. This was a warning to oncoming cars that a biker was in the tunnel. I pushed the button and entered, but there was no shoulder to ride on and it was a nerve-racking ride to daylight at the other end of the dark passageway.

As I crested hills that morning, I looked out over large fog banks hovering above the Pacific waters. Dark monoliths rose out of the fog like mysterious citadels guarding the shore. By the afternoon, the sun had burned off all the vapors and the full beauty of Oregon's coastline was unveiled. I followed beaches where ocean waves lapped at the very edges of the road. Waves thundered against the rocky sentinels offshore, the slow but ceaseless erosion sculpting the unusual pillars of stone called "sea stacks."

Although the route could not be described as mountainous, the hills varied from 200 to 800 feet in elevation. Coming down the hill toward Nehalem Bay, my bike was rolling along at speeds of almost forty miles per hour.

Toward evening, I rode into the town of Tillamook, Oregon. I recognized the name of the town from commercials I'd seen about Tillamook cheese, and my search for a room took me past the cheese factory. It was quite a remarkable sight.

As a businessman, I found the numbers on this operation impressive. A cooperative of 110 dairy farms runs The Tillamook

Cheese Factory. They package one million pounds of cheese every week and can warehouse up to fifty million pounds at different stages of the aging process. Over one million visitors a year stop in to watch the cheese production. Sales are close to $400 million a year. The co-op is especially famous for its Tillamook Cheddar. In 2010, their mild cheddar was awarded the gold medal in the World Cheese Contest in Madison, Wisconsin.

But as a native of Holmes County, I couldn't help but think that even Tillamook's award-winning cheddar couldn't compare to cheese produced in Ohio's Amish Country. I'll take our locally made Swiss over any other cheese in America. We have our own millions of visitors each year who will also attest to the superior tastes coming out of our cheese houses.

Leaving Tillamook, my next goal was the seaside town of Newport, where I was scheduled to meet a friend from long ago. First, though, the route curved inland, through more countryside that looked very much like scenes in my rural area back home. I reveled in familiar sights and smells. Farms and dairy herds abounded. It was like pedaling past the farms of my youth. Large herds of Holsteins grazed along my route, and I stopped at one feedlot and watched the farmer as he unloaded grain for his cattle.

In one field, the arms of a large irrigation sprinkler revolved in a slow rhythm. At a certain point in each revolution, the sunlight hit the water at just the right angle and a rainbow shimmered and then disappeared. I stopped again, watching in fascination as each turn produced a new waterfall of color. *So*, I mused, *this is where rainbows are made.*

The route now veered back toward the coast and took me through the town of Cloverdale, a small hamlet of less than 400 people. Over Memorial Day weekend, Cloverdale's downtown had suffered a devastating fire that spread to a number of structures. Over 100 firefighters from surrounding towns had been called in for assistance, but they were hindered by explosions and a shortage of readily available water. One charred building caught my attention immediately as I rode through town. The local fire station itself had been gutted by the fire.

I realized this was a tragic circumstance for the community, but the irony was inescapable. My mind had nothing to do but wander about all day, and it wondered about that telephone conversation.

"911. What is your emergency?"

"I'd like to report a fire in Cloverdale."

"We will call the fire department immediately."

"It is the fire department that's burning."

So went my imaginary conversation.

My speculations were interrupted by a ringing from my own phone. My friend Andy from Talent, Oregon, was calling to see when I expected to arrive in Newport. He lived sixty miles inland but was planning to drive out to the coast to meet me.

The last time I had seen Andy was the night of that fateful moonlit bike ride. As Ivan and I were pedaling to my cousin's house, Andy passed us in his car and on a whim stopped and chatted for several minutes. I thought little of it at the time; it seemed like just a chance meeting. In all of our journeys, many events seem commonplace and unimportant, scarcely catching our attention. Yet these events weave threads into our stories, threads that can grow into significant and even powerful strands years later. That night on the quiet road, Andy could have passed us by. Instead, he stopped. I would not see him again for over forty-four years. Now this meeting with him, when I was once again pedaling a bicycle, had special meaning for me. He had been a part of the sad night that changed my life.

Andy and I agreed to meet at the Red Door Deli in Newport. I arrived early, so I took a seat in the little deli that did indeed have a huge red door. The red door was standing wide open. As a former restaurant manager I knew that keeping a restaurant door open was an invitation to flies. *Perhaps*, I thought, *the open door gives flies an opportunity to leave?* Suspended from the top of the door frame was a plastic bag full of water. I studied it, but saw only water in a plastic bag, hanging over the doorway. Curiosity got the better of me.

"Excuse me, but why is that plastic bag full of water hanging from your door?"

"It keeps the flies from flying through the opening."

"You mean that actually works?" I asked in disbelief. Apparently the flies are attracted to the bag of water and bump into it and thus are deterred from entering. For twenty-five years in the restaurant business, I had spent a small fortune on sprays, granules, and other strategies of fly destruction. Could it really be true that all I needed was a bag of water over the front entrance?

My enchantment with the fly-repellent system was interrupted by Andy's arrival. After spending several minutes getting reacquainted, we loaded the bike and its burdens into his car and headed inland.

Oregon offers many different terrains. Our route back to my friend's home seemed to consist primarily of hills and curves. Andy attacked these curves with vigor. Had my sense of motion been altered by riding the highway at ten miles per hour, or was he really screaming around those curves too fast?

I'd been invited to stay at Andy's house for the night. Happily, this included a delicious meal cooked by his wife, Lois. Since it was Wednesday and a church night for the Millers, I joined them for an evening service at the Brownsville Mennonite Church.

Along the way, we passed numerous seed farms scattered throughout the Willamette Valley. Grass seed farming is big business here, with over 430,000 acres dedicated to this crop. The grass seed is harvested and taken to a mill, dried, cleaned, and packed for distribution. Huge bales of the straw left behind after the harvest were scattered all over the fields, awaiting transport to a local compactor. The bales would be compacted to half their original size and shipped overseas for animal bedding.

At one time, seed farmers burned off their fields as part of the agricultural cycle. That burning is essential for some types of grass to produce well; burning also controls diseases and pests.

But the environmental folks took offense to the smoke and banned burning on all but 15,000 acres. As a result, many seed farmers must now use more pesticides and chemicals on their fields. That was quite a tradeoff—several days of smoke traded for a lifetime of contaminated water.

After a nourishing breakfast the following morning, Andy took me on a tour through the seed processing plant where he was employed.

That afternoon as we headed back to Newport, he kindly offered to drive me and my bike several miles beyond the city so that I would not have to tangle with the traffic. I declined, telling him how important it was for me to continue my ride from the point where he had picked me up, the precise spot where my bike had stopped rolling the day before at the Red Door Deli. I knew that even a small section skipped would come back to haunt me.

Over the next several days in Oregon, I rode through small coastal towns, parallel to long stretches of beaches, and past miles and miles of large sand dunes piled high by the elements over the ages.

On a big downhill close to Cape Sebastian, I hit my maximum speed for the entire trip, forty-three miles per hour. I also hit a bump in the road that scared some sense into me. That speed was not safe, especially with loaded panniers. I decided that a speed of thirty-five would be the maximum I'd allow the bike to coast; anything faster than that would jeopardize my survival if I had a fall. I found that I had to use the brakes on many downhills, and there was always the temptation to just let the bike fly; but that would have been irresponsible.

Approaching North Bend, I saw another bridge monstrosity in the distance. This one was the Conde B. McCullough Memorial Bridge, a 5,300-foot truss design built in 1936, crossing Coos Bay. Cyclists are advised to walk their bikes across this mile-long bridge; the two lanes are narrow with no shoulder, traffic is heavy, and the winds are strong.

The bridge did have a sidewalk, but it was just wide enough for one pedestrian; squeezing both my bike and myself onto the walkway was difficult. I dropped the bike onto the roadway, and I stayed on the sidewalk. The walkway was almost a foot higher than the road surface, and pushing the bike was awkward. The wind howled furiously. I struggled to keep myself and the bike upright. Were those drivers honking as they passed because they were aggravated at my slow progress, or were they tooting encouragement in my wrestling match with bike and wind?

Things got even worse when I topped the highest portion of the bridge and saw that construction had closed the walking area. I was forced to ride on the roadway for the remainder of the crossing. I hoped those passing drivers who hurled invectives at me were not the Coos Bay welcoming committee.

Crossing scary bridges, however, was not my foremost concern at this time. I was being tortured by my bike seat. Every push of the pedal brought increasing pain. I began to shop for something comfortable to cover that seat.

The road shoulders were a veritable department store that held a bounty of supplies. I'd seen tools of every description scattered along the road. I'd dodged wrenches, tape measures, nuts, bolts, Tupperware containers, hundreds of nails, and shards of wood. It occurred to me that I might find some useful things in this assortment of hard goods and kitchen wares. I started my search for sitting comfort. Anything foam or rubber might work. Pieces of tires were plentiful, but were too big to sit on. Articles of clothing appeared now and then, and for part of a mile I sat on a discarded baby blanket.

At four in the afternoon, I entered Del Norte County and was in California. I was in my third state geographically but in a sad state physically. Although my muscles were acclimating to pedaling many miles, the pain in my posterior filled every biking moment. As I rode into Crescent City, California, I could think of only two things. I needed a tub to soak in, and I needed to find a store to get to the bottom of my bike seat issue. That problem must be solved and behind me before I continued the long trip down the California coast.

I spotted an America's Best Motel with a reasonable rate. Better yet, a brand new pharmacy was just down the street. First would come my relaxing and badly needed soak in the tub. After checking into the motel, I carried my bicycle up a flight of steps and was already dreaming about the relief of a hot soak.

From that night forward, I would always ask before checking in, "Do you have a tub?" This room did not. I was greeted by a bathroom with a small shower unit in the corner. Completely distraught, I threw on my clothes and marched to the front desk to request a room with a tub. To my dismay, I discovered the reason this place had the best prices in town. None of the rooms had a tub.

I returned to my room and surveyed the situation. The shower unit had a raised front panel. Perhaps I could turn the shower into a tub of desperation. The drain was recessed, and a plastic water cup from my room plugged that. Next I wedged my aching body into a u-shape with legs and feet firmly planted against one side and shoulders and head on the other. Holding the shower curtain against the unit's raised front and the side walls, I created a container that held the hot water running over me. Slowly the water level rose, climbing considerably above what I thought possible, contained by a simple shower curtain.

I remembered my mom's days of canning meats and vegetables, and I could still hear the packed mason jars rattling in the canner as the boiling water hissed and steamed on the stove. I felt like one of those ingredients in a canning jar, wedged into a tight spot, simmering and cooking in hot water. Although I didn't hear the little popping sound a jar makes when properly sealed, I knew I was finished when I could no longer move any body parts.

I was packed so tightly into the shower that I needed to roll sideways out onto the tile bathroom floor, and I flopped out along with a considerable amount of water. I slowly unfurled my misshapen body and guessed that the room below me might soon be reporting a plumbing leak somewhere above them.

Feeling considerable relief and quite proud of my ingenuity, I departed for the pharmacy in search of some form of padding.

I did not know what I would find, but I felt confident that tomorrow I would be riding on an added layer of comfort.

The pharmacy aisles held much potential. I briefly considered a hot water bottle. Riding on a thin layer of water would be like sleeping on a water bed, but the head and stopper on the end might create more problems than they solved. All sorts of foam and padded products (including adult diapers) were considered but quickly discarded as too bizarre.

At last I found my solution in the housewares department—Scotch-Brite™ scouring pads. This was a spongy product, covered on one side with a scouring material. The more abrasive side would hold the pads securely between my two layers of biking shorts, and the sponge material would add a layer of comfort. There were four pads in one tightly sealed container. *Perfect*, I thought. One sponge for each hurting cheek plus one backup set.

The next day, I'd be spending my first full day in California. I'd also be fulfilling a lifelong dream, riding through Redwood National Park. I had often tried to imagine what it must be like to stand among those giant trees, and now I would not only be pedaling through them on a bicycle, but I'd do so riding atop Scotch-Brite™ scouring pads.

CHAPTER 6

The Emerald Triangle

Every night I fell into bed bone-tired, thinking, *There is no way this body will have the energy to ride tomorrow.* Somehow a small miracle happened during the night, and muscles and sinews came together, shared nutrients, and agreed to work for another day. A night of rest, a new morning, and I would again be caught up in anticipation of adventure into the unknown.

After my first night of rest in California, I dressed quickly, eager to start the day's route that would take me through Redwood National Park. When I had entered California the day before, Oregon's forests gave way to irrigated fields of vegetables. I was back in farming country and saw many herds of beef and dairy cattle. Just before arriving in Crescent City, I had ridden through Smith River, proclaimed the Easter Lily Capital of the World. But now I was headed toward the giant redwoods, something I had never seen but often tried to imagine.

I was also looking forward to my magic sponge ride. Time to insert those scrubbing sponges! But something was clearly amiss. Moist soap granules covered the scrubbing side, and the sponge side felt damp. The sponges had been presoaked and soaped. My brilliant idea was a complete flop. I briefly considered using the pads anyway, but I glimpsed a possible scenario: I'm riding down the road. A truck approaches. The driver stares in disbelief. He's immediately on his CB, talking about the strangest sight he's ever seen. A bicycle rider's on the highway, and there's a cloud of bubbles enveloping him.

In disgust, I tossed the sponges and my brilliant idea aside. I'm sure the housekeeping staff at the motel has found many strange items left behind by guests, but they are probably still wondering why those four unused Scotch-Brite™ scrubbing pads were left in that room and what caused the water mess in the tubless bathroom.

Leaving Crescent City, I found the Redwood Highway and followed it along the coastline for several hours. Traffic was light and a damp mist blew in from the Pacific Ocean. I was riding through a forest shrouded with fog when an indistinct shape up ahead took my breath away.

The dark giant soared skyward through the gray mist, a sight more incredible than I had ever imagined. The God of creation had certainly worked His majesty here. Words of exclamation failed me as I met my first California redwood tree. I stood in awe and worshipped God that Sunday morning, singing with exhilarated spirit, "Majesty," "How Great Is Our God," and "How Great Thou Art." For a long time I stood at the base of that tree and contemplated the wonder of the worlds His hands had made.

Throughout the morning, other stands of trees captured my attention; but the largest trees were yet to come on the following day, when I would leave the Redwood Highway and ride down the Avenue of the Giants. The magnificent trees, many over 300 feet tall, grow to these large heights due to the constant and abundant moisture drifting in from the ocean. The fog enveloping the redwoods not only waters the trees but also reduces the loss of water through evaporation. These moist conditions allow the redwoods to grow for several thousand years.

The day was filled with incredible natural beauty. It was also a day of constantly changing weather. In the morning, I rode through fog and mist and felt the chill soak into my body. Noonday brought sunshine and favorable wind conditions. A gust of wind traveling in my direction allowed me to hitch up with it.

A tailwind was my best friend on some days of this journey. On occasion, though, that friend became contrary and turned to meet me face to face. My speed would drop to several miles per hour, and all I could do was doggedly pedal through those rough times. But like most good friends, the wind usually worked in my favor.

The favorable wind that day carried me twelve miles past the place I had planned to stop, bringing me to Arcata, California, for the night. This was typical of many days; although I would plan my ride each day, I could never be certain I would end up exactly where I had planned. When I decided to take this ride across America, I knew that God had folks for me to meet, appointments that He wanted me to keep. I have no doubt that Arcata was exactly where God intended me to be that night.

At a restaurant that evening, a fellow in the booth next to mine caught my attention. Something about his demeanor struck a chord with me. Some may call it intuition, but I believe the Holy Spirit within me prompted the conversation we two had that night. The man had led a rough life and had found love and contentment only in the most recent years. Not too long before our meeting, his wife of several years had been thrown off a horse and killed instantly. In his grief, he was trying to make sense of the tragedy.

Our conversation reminded me again that we too often take our loved ones for granted. Cherish your time with your loved ones. If you knew you only had a limited number of days to say or do what needs to be said or done, would you change anything about how you live this day? I will say it for you: Your time is limited and the moments are trickling away...

The next morning started with a ride around the cloverleaf entrance to Route 101. I joined hundreds of cars and trucks, just another person on the highway of life, starting a new day. I knew another day of redwoods was ahead of me and the town of Eureka was my morning destination, but I was pedaling into another day of unknown adventure.

Just outside of Eureka I pulled off the road, amazed at the vast amount of lumber stacked around the California Redwood Lumber Company. Over thirty types of redwood boards are stocked there, sorted by grade and durability.

In downtown Eureka, I passed folks carrying full garbage bags over their shoulders. First glance might note the unkempt appearance of many of these people and characterize them as undesirable. I didn't sense a story until after I had passed a recycling building and realized that was where these folks were going with their loaded bags. Curiosity got the better of me. I wheeled my bicycle around.

A car had pulled to the side of the street. The interior was filled with rubbish, and a couple worked at emptying the trunk of bottles and cans. The man's long black hair hung down over his face as he stooped over the sidewalk, filling garbage bags with the empty cans. I propped my bicycle against the wall of the building.

"Hey, man, can I help you with those?" I asked.

He looked at me skeptically. "Why would you want to?"

I explained that I was on a cross-country bike ride and was just curious about the goings-on here. He introduced himself as Joey.

"Folks collect cans over the weekend and bring them here for some money. As you can probably tell, most of them are addicted to drugs and need drug money. My wife and I are unemployed and homeless and have lived the past three years in a local campground, but this morning the cops came and chased all of us out." He went on to tell me that some drug activity had been going on at the campground, and so every squatter living there had been expelled. He and his wife had gathered all the bottles and cans they could find and brought them here for some cash.

"How much will you get for this carload?" I asked. He estimated a payment of $35. "What will you do now?" I wanted to know.

"We'll park the car somewhere for three days, then try to sneak back into the campground."

I helped Joey carry his bounty into the processing center where bottles and cans were weighed and separated. As I left, I thought about how fortunate we are in Amish Country. People who find themselves destitute and homeless might be in those circumstances because of their own bad decisions or circumstances beyond their control. But whatever the reasons for their sad situation, they must have no support system whatsoever. Here in Amish Country, we have roots. We have several generations of family who care about us. We have churches that want to help. Granted, folks in small towns probably know more about you than you really want them to know—but isn't that better than having no one who cares?

I had just settled back into pedaling rhythm when I was stopped again, this time by an aroma that carried me back to boyhood. It was the aroma of food. But this was not people food; instead, it was familiar smells floating from the huge feed mill on my right. Before I started a career of feeding hungry humans, my dad had already worked forty years feeding livestock. He worked in a grain mill, and I spent many days as a young lad roaming about the Mount Hope Elevator, where he was employed. I'd ride with Dad as he made his rounds picking up and delivering grain at the Amish farms. While Dad shoveled grain, I was off admiring the vast beams or the large sandstone foundations of the Amish barns.

I could not resist. I wandered about the Nilsen Company, exploring sights and aromas, listening to the familiar hum of machinery, transported back to another time and place.

Earlier that morning, Eureka had been just a name on the map. Now it was images of drug addicts and homeless people scrounging for a few dollars contrasted with the smells and sounds that took me back to a safe and innocent childhood.

And Eureka had one more memorable picture for me. Leaving town, I met a bicycle rider who had attached a large set of antlers to his handlebars. The buckcycle rider had a long beard that reminded me of my Amish Country neighbors. He certainly wouldn't want to be riding that bicycle through our county during deer season.

Shortly past the town of Del Rio, I exited onto the Avenue of the Giants. This section of road is the old Highway 101 and parallels

Route 101 for thirty-one miles. The road is very narrow and the giant redwoods crowd in on both sides of the roadway.

I stopped and toured The Famous One-Log House. In the early 1900s, a man felled a giant redwood that was supposedly 2,100 years old. Over eight months' time, he carved a bedroom, kitchen, and living room out of a thirty-two-foot section of the tree trunk. Another enterprising fellow had purchased the one-log house and wheeled it about to fairs and festivals, charging a small admission to see the wonder. It now has a permanent home at a gift shop, where, for a dollar donation, I was allowed to walk through the cozy interior. It does give a new meaning to the term "tree house."

My fascination with the massive redwood trees must end, since I still had many miles to reach my goal of Garberville, California. Climbing several large hills seemed more difficult than usual; I was feeling weaker and the torture of my bike seat grew worse with each passing minute.

Both issues were soon resolved. Ripe blackberries were growing alongside the road, and I stopped for a few refreshing handfuls of the sweet fruit. As I rested, I noticed the vines with broad leaves intertwining the berry bushes. Could those broad leaves be used to cushion my ride? Hoping they were not of a poisonous variety, I plucked a handful and inserted them where I had planned to lodge my Scotch-Brite™ pads. The greenery was not as helpful as those scrubbing sponges might have been, I decided; but nevertheless, it was a little fluff for my duff, a little viney for the hiney.

Garberville was a throwback to the hippie sixties era. Many long-haired folks roamed the main street. I was in an area known as The Emerald Triangle. The three counties of Humboldt, Mendocino, and Trinity are the largest producers of marijuana in the United States. Over 1,000 growers have patches of cannabis scattered about the three counties, and it appeared that many consumers of this product had stationed themselves in Garberville.

My most immediate need was my soak; then I would search for food. From my motel window, I spotted a nearby Italian restaurant and made that my dining choice.

Although not a fancy establishment by any standards, the place was catering to the needs of high society folks. Well, perhaps not so much society folks as just plain high folks. No one seemed attuned to the fact that there was no service. While I waited for a server, I did my daily journaling. That done, I finally walked to the front desk and inquired about the possibility of service. The manager explained that he had several employees call off and was in a hopeless meltdown mode. "Please leave and go to another restaurant down the street," he advised me. Since I had been on his side of several restaurant meltdowns myself, I had great sympathy for the man and did take my leave.

The second restaurant had no service, either; it also did not have a manager willing to tell me they didn't have service. I finally joined the long line of high-minded folks at a nearby Subway and awaited my meal.

I have been told I lack patience. One thing all these dread-locked youth seemed to have was patience. Perhaps patience is a side effect of that wild weed growing all over this area. California has passed a law legalizing the growth of medical marijuana. With a doctor's signature confirming that you have an affliction and that marijuana might benefit you, you can legally raise and use the product. Could a person with an acute case of impatience get a script? In California, the answer is probably yes.

Back in my room, I savored my sandwich and made a call to my friends Joy and Alan in Novato, California. Joy is a friend from many years ago; she had invited me to stop at their home near San Francisco. She is also the owner of the Berlin Natural Bakery in Amish Country, running that business from her home on the west coast. I planned to take a day off, getting reacquainted with Joy and Alan and visiting local bike shops in hopes of finding a more comfortable bike seat.

Until then, my search continued for something to cushion my ride. By now I realized I didn't need to stop at a store; everything necessary for survival was available on America's shoulder. My bike had dodged coats and shoes, unopened cans of fruit, even the back end of a deer decoy. I occasionally stopped pedaling to pick up coins; and when the sun shone, I applied lip balm found in my roadside pharmacy. I stashed away an almost-new screwdriver, thinking it might be useful. Here in the Emerald Triangle, hundreds of hypodermic needles lay scattered along the highway.

A blue trucker's glove caught my eye. Constructed of a thick rubber material, it fit quite nicely over the bicycle seat. Its five blue digits fluttered in the breeze as I sailed down the highway. I could imagine some child questioning a parent. *How does that man ride when he's sitting on his hand? Oh, look, Mom. His fingers have all turned blue.*

Three miles short of Piercy, California, I needed a break and pulled over at Confusion Hill, a tourist trap promoting a house that defied gravity. I tossed my blue glove over the handlebars and gave in to curiosity.

A small, ramshackle structure had been built into the hillside at a point where water supposedly ran uphill, down was up, and the laws of gravity were somehow suspended or even reversed. I knew I was about to become another gullible sucker, but I parted with $5 to satisfy my curiosity. The admission was $4.99 more than the sight was worth; I immediately realized that the odd angles of the shoddy construction gave it the appearance of defying gravity. I was sorry to have been separated from my five dollar bill, but grudgingly admired the hucksterism it took to pull folks in off the highway for something so outlandish.

What really astonished me was that some folks actually believed there was a mysterious power at that spot. I will admit, though, there were times in California when I myself questioned whether natural laws had somehow gone awry. Those were the times I thought my bike was headed downhill, but I found myself pedaling a gradual uphill instead.

But strange things do happen in a triangle, as illustrated by the Bermuda Triangle off our east coast. The Emerald Triangle held one more bizarre encounter for me. Somewhere between Leggett and Laytonville, I pulled off the highway for another break. I was in a wooded area with many lanes leading up into the surrounding hills. Ominous chains and padlocks blocked access to the lanes and warned me to stay on the highway; I got the message, squashing any whims of curiosity. I did, though, position myself at the end of one gravel driveway, lying on my back with both legs pointing skyward.

The crunch of tires on gravel jerked me out of my repose. A gruff voice demanded full attention. The young man standing over me had a large knife strapped to his chest.

"What are you doing here?" he asked.

"I'm just resting, taking a break from my bike ride," I replied. Realizing I was no threat, he calmed down and told me I was in the heart of marijuana territory. Those lanes led to patches in the hills, and the young man made it clear that folks would not hesitate to kill to protect their crop. I assured him I was neither the law nor an intruder but just a biker passing through. He warned me to be careful. His parting remark was, "We look out for each other out here."

In Laytonville, I stopped at a small grocery store for a snack. A fellow was lounging outside the store and I asked him about industry in the area.

"We farm marijuana."

"Isn't that illegal?"

"It used to be illegal, and that was when we really made money here. Then they passed a law allowing a certain amount of plants for medicinal purposes, and most of us growers now have permits allowing us to grow twenty-five plants. Of course, we plant many more than that." He grinned.

"How much can you make on twenty-five plants?"

"About $75,000." I told him about my encounter with the man several miles out of town.

"Someone saw you stopped there and called the owner. Those hills are filled with patches of weed and whenever someone strange shows up, we get nervous. The federal government still outlaws marijuana, even though the state allows it.

"We'd actually prefer it to be illegal; we'd make more money. Now, with medical permits so easy to get, we have lots of competition. And now they're even trying to legalize marijuana completely here in California. That would absolutely kill our business."

My education about this hemp product had gone further than I had ever thought necessary, but it gave me much to think about. As with so many things in life, you need to follow the money trail to get to the heart of any issue. Marijuana was outlawed at one time to "protect" our society. It's ironic that now the people who will profit the most from keeping this wild weed illegal are the growers, the mob, the smugglers, and the dealers.

I have no doubt that there are medical benefits to this plant. I do believe that in God's nature there are cures for every type of illness; we just have not yet discovered all of those natural secrets. When my wife was undergoing chemotherapy for cancer, one drug used was derived from taxol, found in the bark of the Pacific yew.

And while I won't denigrate anyone who does benefit from marijuana's medicinal value, I also believe most users are simply attempting to alter their state of mind. Our society is under great stress. Folks look for an escape from reality. Sadly, many turn to drugs and alcohol for a temporary high.

I believe the only remedy for society's ills is a personal relationship with Jesus Christ. The only spirit necessary for my natural highs is the Holy Spirit dwelling within me. Some folks might question whether a Christian should indulge in the ornery sense of humor that often pops into my discourse, but my relationship with an almighty God makes it possible to look beyond pain and see humor in most situations.

I believe, too, that as a son of God I am heir to every part of the country that I traveled on this journey. God owns quite a piece of real estate, and I was inspecting my inheritance and talking to my Father about everything I found. This corner of the universe, I reported, needed some maintenance. There was a weed here and there that needed plucking.

On the outskirts of Willits, I was startlcd by two dogs that took offense to my passage. Dogs are a menace to riders. Spotting a dog along the path is always cause for some anxiety; you never know how territorial the animal may be. The best plan is to hammer the pedals as hard as possible and outrun any dog you meet.

This was my first encounter with canines on this ride. The big hound gave only a perfunctory chase and quickly returned to his yard. The smaller one had visions of grandeur. Perhaps it wanted to impress with its determination. Its chase was clearly futile, so I felt safe in encouraging the little thing to run harder and even hurled a few insults at my dogged pursuer. I suspect the little critter actually thought it scared me away.

The chase did hasten my arrival into Willits. I arrived without the blue fingers. Earlier that afternoon, I had been gliding downhill when I rose from my seat briefly to change positions. My blue rubber glove took this momentary lapse on my part as opportunity to jump on the breeze and take flight. It had served me well, but I did not wish to pedal back uphill to retrieve it.

I had Plan B stashed away in one of my panniers. That morning, I had spotted a foam coffee-cup holder lying on the shoulder. It looked like a fitting candidate for the spot between my two layers of biking shorts. I picked it up and stashed it away. The cup holder and my new slotted screwdriver would both be useful in the days to come.

CHAPTER 7

Bobby White

God works in mysterious ways, an old hymn tells us. This day would remind me of that once again.

Each morning I'd squeeze my bike tires to make certain they were properly inflated for the day's journey. In Willits that morning, I found the back tire completely flat. My spirit was also deflated at the thought of removing that back tire and having to contend with the greasy chain and all those gears.

Hoping to ride to a bike shop and let them repair the tire, I did a quick Internet search and found a shop in town and two more in the next town, Ukiah. It was six o'clock, and the shop in Willits would not open for another two hours; I could be twenty to thirty miles down the road by then. Across the street from my motel was a service station with an air pump. I decided to inflate the tire and take a chance that it would take me the twenty miles to Ukiah.

After inflating the tire, I returned to my motel room to load up the bike. Before starting out, though, I wanted to know the severity of the leak. I combined soap and water in the sink and rubbed the foamy mixture over the rear tire. Sure enough, a little pile of bubbles appeared, but it was a very slow leak. I felt safe in my decision to ride on to the next town.

While I had slept that night and the air was slowly seeping from my tire, another bike rider was having his own tire problems. On Route 20, Bobby White was riding through the night from Fort Bragg to Willets; then he, like me, would be headed down Route 101 to Ukiah, California. Because of two flat tires, a most amazing encounter took place.

Over the past several days I'd been climbing higher in elevation; I was now looking forward to my reward, an extended downhill. First, though, one final climb.

A short distance ahead of me, a rider labored up the hill. He was on a small twenty-six-inch bike, burdened with a large backpack and pedaling slowly. It was an odd sight; the bike was much too small for him, and his legs bowed out as if he were riding a pony.

As I neared the top of the hill, I saw that the rider had stopped at a small rest area. Concerned about his well-being, I asked if he needed help.

"No, I'm just taking a short rest break."

That was fine with me. His appearance set him apart from most riders I'd met along my journey. His clothes were dirty and his disheveled hair was tied back in a ponytail. Back home, this would be a person we would hope is only traveling through; we might graciously wish him well, but we would not want him to find our community so pleasant that he would decide to stay. Back in God's country, this man would have been the topic of conversation at our little corner tables in the restaurants. The talk would be about that long-haired and dirty bicycle rider wandering around the community. I was relieved he didn't need my help. I'd been courteous, but I intended to pass him by and never see him again.

Okay, I will admit that often I have been far too judgmental. That is one consequence of growing up in such an insulated community. Anything or anyone different from what we know is regarded with a critical and skeptical eye. While I hiked the Appalachian Trail, I was outside the safe cocoon of Holmes County and God had many lessons for me, teaching me through my discomfort. Apparently I still had some learning to do; here was yet another training session God felt I needed.

I had topped the hill and was enjoying the exhilaration of the extended downhill coast when I suddenly squeezed the brakes and slid to a stop. Money!

The morning after my century ride, as I pedaled through the streets of Aberdeen, Washington, I had spotted a dime on the street. I stopped and picked it up and decided to pocket any coin or paper money I might find on my trip. How much might I accumulate while riding across the entire country? I've done this for a number of years in Holmes County, and pennies are, of course, the most common denomination found. A dime gets me excited and quarters absolutely bring euphoria. Every discovery is stashed away; and on New Year's Day, I count my yearly finds and then dump the pile into a container holding many years of roadside and sidewalk wealth. Someday, some unfortunate bank teller will be given the task of sorting through all the scratched and weather-worn treasure.

Now, on a downhill scoot at thirty miles per hour, I had caught a glint of silver on the shoulder. This was the mother lode of treasure, three quarters and one dime. While I gathered up my filthy lucre, the biker I had just met passed me and inquired if I needed help.

"No, just picking up some coins," I said.

Pedaling again, I quickly caught up with the little bike. Conversation was now unavoidable.

I discovered this rider was also heading to Ukiah, and I explained my tire problem and asked if he knew where the bike shops were located. He was riding into Ukiah for a court hearing and would be happy to guide me in the right direction. I offered to buy him breakfast if he would lead me to one of the shops.

For the next fifteen miles we rode side by side. He seemed to tire easily, and we stopped several times so that he could rest. When I told him about my ride across America seeking God-ordained meetings, he inquired if I was a Christian. I said yes. He pointed to his shirt that pictured a dove being released by two outstretched hands and exclaimed, "I'm a Christian, too!"

I admit that I was a little surprised. Then he told me his incredible story.

His name was Bobby White and he had been a soldier in Desert Storm in 1991. His vehicle was hit by enemy fire, and life-threatening injuries kept him in the hospital for many months. Discharged from the military, he was sent home in a wheelchair. The doctors told him he would probably never walk again.

Returning home paralyzed, angry, and bitter, he drowned his troubles in alcohol and spent most evenings away from his family. His life continued on a downward spiral until his wife eventually divorced him and moved away, taking their daughter with her.

A friend took him to a Christian concert one night, and he heard the good news about God sending his Son Jesus to die for Bobby White. Realizing and admitting his desperate need for redemption, Bobby gave his life to Christ. He began to attend a local Bible-believing church. When he became convinced that God could heal him, he promised God that if he was ever able to walk again, he would ride a bicycle everywhere he went and would proclaim God's love to anyone he met.

Bobby changed his diet, took herbal medications, did physical therapy daily, and prayed and praised God for the healing he was receiving. After eight months of his new regimen and believing for a miracle, he walked again. He had been in the wheelchair for eight years.

Keeping his promise to God, he purchased a new bicycle and a small bike trailer in which to carry his belongings when he traveled. Having no need for the wheelchair, he painted it gold, turned it into a planter, and placed it on his front lawn for everyone to see.

Bobby was now bothered greatly by the profanities used constantly by his buddies. He welded together an arch and placed it over his golden wheelchair planter. Letters on the arch read, GOD'S LAST NAME ISN'T D—N. He also anointed his door frame; and every time he entered or left his house, he prayed the blood of Christ over that door. On the outside of the frame he posted a sign that stated, BEWARE, IF YOU HAVE EVIL INTENTS OR EVIL THOUGHTS. DOOR FRAME IS ANOINTED.

One day an especially profane neighbor paid a visit. As he entered Bobby's house, he fell to his knees. Dumbfounded at his unexpected collapse, he looked up at Bobby White and exclaimed, "Something's wrong with me!"

"You just walked through my anointed door frame and God has struck you down," replied Bobby. "You will never use God's name in vain again. You need to give your life to God right this minute."

The man broke down. With tears running down his face, he confessed he was a sinner: And on Bobby White's floor, by the anointed door frame, that profane neighbor accepted Jesus Christ.

Bobby was riding beside me. As he remembered the day his neighbor was saved, he gestured emphatically with outstretched hand and exclaimed passionately, "*I got him!*" Then he added, "That is, God did!"

We neared the exit to Ukiah and suspended our conversation as we rolled into town. It was a beautiful morning and young people, many with dreadlocked hair, were already out and about. Many of them were openly smoking a product that would get folks arrested in most towns of America. I suspected they all had medical maladies of one sort or another, requiring a certain permit to obtain the medication. But the malady was not one of rudeness, unfriendliness, or disrespect. There were welcoming waves and warm smiles as we rode down the street toward the bike shop.

While waiting for the mechanic to install a new, heavy-duty tire tube on my bike, Bobby and I went in search of a restaurant; I wanted to fulfill my promise to him. Following a prayer from Bobby that included everyone within earshot, our conversation continued.

Several months ago, he had gone to Willits for an event and had parked his bicycle and trailer behind the backstop of the town ballpark. When he returned for his bike, he was attacked by three meth addicts. Methamphetamine is a highly addictive drug responsible for many violent crimes. I told him about all the hypodermic needles I'd seen along the roadside the previous day.

"The marijuana users are harmless; no one's afraid of them," Bobby said. "But these meth users are completely insane. Those three addicts attacked me and beat me and stabbed me. They took my bike and trailer and all my money and left me for dead."

Bobby lay there until his battered body was discovered by a woman walking her dog. The dog found him and barked until its owner came to investigate. Medics were called, but their first thought was that he was already dead; then someone detected a small movement. At the hospital, doctors removed half of Bobby's lung; that explained his frequent rest stops and gasping breaths as we biked.

After his release from the hospital, Bobby was very angry and withdrawn. He rejected offers of assistance from his church family and sank into deep self-pity.

"But I just got so tired of pitying myself that I couldn't tolerate who I'd become," he told me. One morning in church, under conviction about his anger and bitterness, he stood to his feet during the sharing time and addressed the congregation. He apologized for his anger, and with tears streaming down his face asked their forgiveness for rejecting their offers of help.

The three addicts were eventually arrested and were in prison awaiting trial. Bobby was on his way to testify against them. One of the three had already been in prison three times, but had been released every time. The last stint had been incarceration in San Quentin. He had murdered someone, but was released on a technicality.

"He's already killed one person and got away with it." Friends of Bobby's assailants had threatened to harm him if he testified, but he was determined to go to court. "If I don't do my part to put them in prison, they'll do this to someone else. I'm not afraid of dying anyway; it's living that scares me," Bobby told me.

Bobby White's only income was a monthly disability check from the government. His court date was looming and he had no transportation to Ukiah, since his stolen bike was never recovered. He spent $5 at a local junk yard and purchased a twenty-six-inch broken bike frame, two twenty-six-inch knobby tires and several other bike parts. He welded the parts together into what he called his "twenty-six-inch knobby bike." That satisfied my curiosity about the small bike he was riding. On this bike, he set out for Ukiah.

"Early this morning, while I was riding up Route 20 from the coast, my front tire blew out," he told me. But he was prepared. In that big, heavy backpack he carried an extra tube, a roll of duct tape, and another set of clothes for his court appearance. Trying to fix that tire in the dark was difficult, but he did manage to insert the new tube.

Then another problem arose. Not only had the tube exploded, but it had also blown a hole in the tire. A gaping tear allowed the inflated inner tube to bulge out. He wound duct tape around the aneurysm and managed to hold the tube inside the tire.

Relieved that he had been prepared for these emergencies, he attempted to continue his ride. But he was abruptly stopped. The duct tape wound around and around the tire created a thickness that would not pass under the brake pads.

Bobby was devastated and desperate. He raised his face to the sky and pleaded with God for help. "God, if I'm to make this court date today, it's now in your hands; I don't know what to do."

In the early morning light, he saw a pickup coming down the road. It pulled over and a young man stepped out of the truck.

"Sir, do you need help?" the truck driver asked.

"Yes. I'm in trouble here. I need a front tire for my bicycle." Half in jest, Bobby asked if he might have a twenty-six-inch tire lying in the back of his truck.

"Take a look," the young man said. "I stop and pick up all kinds of stuff I find along the highway. You never know when you might need something."

Bobby took a look. To his incredulous surprise, a new twenty-six-inch knobby bicycle tire lay in the middle of the truck bed.

"Didn't even remember it was there. Must have picked it up somewhere, though," said the young driver.

"I don't have any money to buy it," said Bobby.

"There's no charge. Take it—it's yours," said the truck driver. Bobby retrieved the tire and the truck sped away. It was an early morning miracle, and he thanked and praised God while he changed the tire.

Sitting there and listening to Bobby's story, I was stunned. It was clear that God had used two flat tires that morning to synchronize our days so that we two would meet. How often we are inconvenienced by some unexpected turn and in our frustration we fail to see that God may be setting up a divine occasion. Had my tire not been flat that morning, I would have missed this encounter with one of the most inspiring folks I have ever met.

After picking up my own bicycle, I thanked Bobby for his testimony and story. He invited me to stop and visit his home on coastal Highway 1.

"I have ten acres facing the ocean that my father willed to me when he passed away several years ago. There's a small house with a great view over the ocean. My gold wheelchair reminds me how fortunate I am to be enjoying God's blessings." Bobby had endured more pain and heartache than any one person should be asked to carry, yet he rejoiced in what little he had.

Back home in our sheltered community, we are fortunate and blessed, not only with the lovely landscape that is Holmes County but with good jobs, schools, and churches. I know of no one who is collecting cans for a few meager dollars to pay for their next meal. No one is sleeping under bridges because they are homeless in Amish Country. No one I know has been beaten and robbed by meth addicts.

We are blessed because our community was created by ancestors who honored God and our grandparents and parents passed that godly heritage on to us. Folks by the millions realize there is something compelling about our community. Sure, they come for the scenery, the food, the crafts, the peaceful lodging. But there is something else drawing them. I believe it is our people. We have something they desire—a slower lifestyle, a sense of contentment, a peace. Sadly, most will leave without hearing about the peace that passes all understanding.

As I pedaled away from Bobby and the bike shop, I was still thinking about the amazing story I had heard that day. The Spirit within had nudged me about many things. I was reminded that God does work for what is best in our lives. I was reminded that God's children do not all look exactly like me. The inspiration and instruction came through someone I would probably have avoided if left to my own plan. I was reminded to be grateful for my home and heritage.

You may be the person who can make a difference in someone else's life. The next time you are having a frustrating day and it seems that nothing is falling into place, be patient and watchful; a divine encounter may be just around the corner. Would I have met Bobby White if there had been no flat tires? Was everything that day just coincidence? Do encounters like this just randomly happen? What about the improbability of a pickup truck coming by in the early morning with a twenty-six-inch bicycle tire in the back? Might Bobby's benefactor have been an angel? Do you think angels could be driving pickup trucks?

I do know what I believe, but I still have some unanswered questions myself. Of this one thing I am sure, though: God does move in mysterious ways, His wonders to perform.

CHAPTER 8

Caples Lake Caper

Finding a route across America should not be too difficult, right? The many highways and byways crisscrossing our country would surely make it easy to travel from one point to another. As I planned my bike journey, I had a general idea of the route I wanted to take—down the west coast, then inland and east—but I wasn't too concerned about finding my way from one town to another. The reality, however, was quite different. Some roads that led toward my next destination were unwelcoming and even forbidding.

While pedaling into Cloverdale, California, I spotted a sign at the entrance to the on ramp prohibiting bicycles on the next stretch of Highway 101. In my room that evening, I researched Route 101 and discovered there were sections that were designated as interstate highways. I had already pedaled some of those sections, but my ignorance had ruled the day and my lawbreaking was quite unintentional.

Now, with the knowledge that I would be breaking the law if I continued on the same road, I went in search of information. At a service station, someone told me about an old road called the Old Redwood Highway. It ran somewhat parallel to 101 and would be my new route in the morning.

In the faint, early morning light, I found my new old highway. I was in Sonoma County and entering wine country. Over 150 wineries dot the landscape in Sonoma. On either side of me stretched long rows of grapevines. Some rows marched straight across the countryside; other rows meandered around slopes and valleys.

I rode through the small communities of Asti, Geyserville, and Healdsburg. The meticulously manicured wineries took me back several years to another time and a memory that still makes me smile.

It was the year before my wife passed away. We were in Napa Valley with my youngest daughter and her husband, and I had been regaling them with stories of my youth and some of my mischievous adventures. My daughter had said wistfully that she didn't have memories of such childhood escapades. I told her that my childhood list of forbidden things had been so long that it actually became a challenge for me to discover and explore as many of those things as I could.

"You didn't have those prohibitions; you had freedoms I didn't have." What irony! The life that had felt so restrictive to me now seemed appealing to my daughter.

We had already visited several other wineries when we approached the Robert Mondavi Winery. I recognized the name and decided to make this our final tour. While my family browsed the gift shop, I noticed a door leading to a small garden. Being somewhat allergic to gift shops, I decided to check out the surroundings.

Beyond a terraced garden was a large, ornate doorway with a sign prohibiting visitors. PRIVATE AREA, NO VISITORS BEYOND THIS POINT, it read. However, the message relayed to my brain was PROCEED AT YOUR OWN RISK. There had to be something special back there, and I was curious what it might be. I decided that asking for forgiveness later rather than permission now was the proper way to proceed.

The doorway led to a building with private wine-tasting rooms. Long and elaborately carved wooden tables graced these rooms, and locked glass cabinets held rare wines. This was obviously where the rich and famous met to sample expensive wine and convince each other of their importance. What caught my eye, though, was a familiar figure walking towards me. I recognized her as Maria Shriver Kennedy, the niece of President Kennedy and the wife of the governor of California, Arnold Schwarzenegger. And I surmised that if Maria was here, the governor might be present also.

My daughter would want to be a part of this adventure. I hurried back to the gift shop and reminded her of our conversation that morning.

"Here's your chance for an adventure. Follow me," I told her. She and her husband both followed me out through the garden. Then she spotted that obnoxious sign.

"It says no one's allowed back here," she said with some hesitation.

"It means nothing. Keep following."

We rounded a corner and came face to face with the governor of California, his wife, and their family. Granted, several burly security guards were also in attendance. But before the guards could deter me, I asked Arnold if he had ever met an Amish man from Ohio. Okay, I might have misrepresented myself, but I'm sure the governor knew that I did not look like an Amish man. My question was enough to get his attention, though.

"Ahh, Cuhlumbus," he said with his Austrian accent. "That's one of my favorite cities; and Ohio is my second favorite state, next to California." He had one of his sons take a picture as he posed with me and my daughter and son-in law. The governor seemed genuinely happy to talk with us; the wife, not so much. I offered to show him around Amish Country the next time he came to Ohio. I am still waiting for him to call.

Pedaling through wine country and thinking about those good memories reminded me again how quickly life can change. Today, your family is intact and all is well; but that can all change in a heartbeat. We must cherish each day we have with each other. We really only have today to tell our loved ones how much they mean to us. Treasure those memories you make with your families. Someday you, too, may be on a journey where those good memories will sustain you.

My trip down memory lane had taken me to Santa Rosa, where I looked for the Petaluma Hill Road. This side road took me to Petaluma, but in that town I encountered a dilemma. My destination for day's end was Novato, where I'd take some time off to rest at Joy and Alan's house. The route from Petaluma to Novato began with a six-mile stretch of interstate highway.

There was no other choice, no side roads, no Plan B. I was forced to make a dash down the interstate highway. The sign prohibiting bikers flashed past me as I zoomed down the on ramp. The traffic was heavy, but the shoulder was wide. I pedaled as fast as I could.

I saw the problem in the distance, a long bridge with no shoulder. I pulled to the side of the road and watched the traffic, waiting for a gap between vehicles that would be big enough for me to dart into the traffic flow and onto the bridge. At last a small opening appeared; and with a quick prayer for safety, I entered the fray.

Horns blasting all around me confirmed I was unwelcome and in unfriendly territory. The ride was harrowing. I pedaled furiously and arrived on the other side, safe but shaken. I rode several more miles at breakneck speed, until the divided highway merged and I knew I was riding legally again.

By midafternoon I reached the outskirts of Novato. I still needed to maneuver through merging traffic at eight exit ramps before I reached the exit for Joy and Alan's house and a much-needed rest.

At my friends' home, I enjoyed a hot shower, Coke, chocolate cake, steak, and potatoes. More, I relished the company and conversation of friends. Loneliness had begun to shadow me as I pedaled alone every day.

I was still thirty miles from San Francisco. The traffic would only get worse as I approached that city, and I wanted to find an alternate, safer route to the Golden Gate Bridge. My dream of biking across that magnificent edifice was one of the reasons I included San Francisco on my trip.

The next morning, Alan, Joy, and I spent several hours driving through small communities, charting a route to San Francisco and the Golden Gate Bridge.

The second morning at my friends' home, I climbed back on my bike and headed toward the famous bridge. San Francisco is built on a series of hills, and I meandered up and down narrow roads leading through quaint little clusters of homes. Houses seem to be stacked on the hillsides; down on the bay, people live in little houseboats.

My plan was to bike across the Golden Gate Bridge and then Alan and Joy would pick me up and return me to their home for one more night. Several nights in a nice house, rest in a soft bed, good food, and the company of friends was more than I could resist.

The ride across the Golden Gate did not disappoint. Although I detest riding across bridges, this one has a large, enclosed sidewalk for bikers and pedestrians. I was filled with awe at the giant orange structure. Fog enveloped the tops of the towers that hold the giant cables. I could see Alcatraz out in the bay, the famous prison perched atop the rocky island.

I dodged gawking tourists and arrived safely on the south side of the bridge. From a parking lot there, a street curves down and under the end of the span. I looped through the area under the bridge, acquainting myself with the streets. The next morning I would be dropped off here, and I wanted to make certain I started my ride at the precise spot I had ended it after crossing the bridge.

Back at the house, I emptied my panniers and chose items to send home. Anything that was not absolutely essential must go. I had been carrying thirty pounds and was able to lighten my load by twelve pounds.

At a local bike shop, I inquired about a less miserable seat. The shop owner sold me an expensive seat; he had used the same model himself. Ridden over 5,000 miles with no discomfort, he insisted. Judging by my ensuing experience with that seat, he stretched the truth by 4,995 miles.

That evening, Alan warned me that I might have a problem leaving San Francisco the following morning. The San Francisco Marathon was scheduled that day, and 24,000 runners would be stampeding along the same route I would take from the Golden Gate Bridge to the San Francisco ferry terminal at Pier 41. I planned to cross San Francisco Bay on the ferry, a one-hour ride to Vallejo, California.

Early the following morning, we drove across the bridge again and Alan dropped me and my bike at the opposite end. I said good-bye to my friend, jumped on my bike, and coasted down the street that curved beneath the bridge.

My coast ended and I leaned into the pedals. But something was amiss. The pedals would not move. While the bicycle lay in the back of Alan's van, the chain had dropped off the front gear and was now wedged tightly between the gear and the frame. I tugged and pulled to no avail. I needed a tool to pry the chain loose.

"The screwdriver!" I very nearly yelled. I had spotted a screwdriver several days before and had already passed it by when something within me said, *You're going to need that.* I had turned my bike around, picked up the screwdriver, and stowed it in my pannier. It now rescued me from my predicament in the bowels of the Golden Gate Bridge.

Arriving at the spot where I had concluded my ride the previous day, I encountered the runners, thousands of them. The first six miles along Fisherman's Wharf was closed to vehicle traffic. It was the route I wanted to take to the ferry terminal, and I explained my dilemma to a policeman standing guard. He allowed me to proceed, but warned me to be very cautious. For the next hour, I was a salmon going upstream as I faced those 24,000 runners. It was quite a task avoiding both the runners and the discarded water cups littering the street.

Just past Fisherman's Wharf, I saw Pier 39, where my family had departed on a visit to Alcatraz Island the day after our visit with the governor. But that was then and this was now, and I needed to get to Pier 41 for my ride. With ten minutes to spare, I bought my ticket and arrived in Vallejo an hour later.

My journey took on a new direction, a direction that filled me with joy. I was now pedaling east, riding in the direction of home. My route from Vallejo took me inland through farming country toward my goal for the evening, Sacramento, ninety miles distant.

I was riding parallel to I-680 on Lopes Road. As if getting tangled up in a marathon wasn't enough excitement for one day, I now rode into a bicycle race. My intended route was filled with racing bikes of all kinds and descriptions. Fancy wheels flashed as riders bent into the wind, their colorful outfits all tagged with racing numbers. Tents and booths set up along the route catered to the needs of the racers, and folks lined the streets, cheering on their favorites.

With a warning from an official to be very cautious, I joined the fray. In the midst of this group of gazelles lumbered one biker encumbered by two loaded panniers. *What number are you?* spectators yelled at me. I held up my index finger and declared I was number one, slightly exaggerating my importance.

As I progressed inland, headed toward Sacramento and the mountain pass to Nevada, I rode along miles of avocado groves. Those gave way to fields of tomatoes and other vegetables.

The day was extremely hot. At a small café surrounded by rows of grapes, I stopped for refreshment and struck up a conversation with two cyclists out on a day ride. They were familiar with the area; and when they learned I was headed to Sacramento, they advised me to stay near the historical district of Old Town Sacramento, rather than where I had planned to stop in West Sacramento.

Several hours later, while passing through Fairfield, California, I took another rest break at a grassy area in front of a strip mall parking lot. A fence separated me from the parking area, but

73

I recognized familiar voices. The same two men I had met previously had parked their vehicles here while they biked. Another conversation ensued, and they told me about a twenty-five-mile bike path connecting Sacramento to Folsom, California. I had read about the bike path, but didn't know where to find it. And what a great relief to know I would not be fighting traffic on the morrow.

It was one hot and tired biker that arrived in Sacramento late that night. Based on my conversations with the two bikers, I was looking for the area called Old Sacramento. While pedaling down Capitol Avenue, I spotted the capitol building where my buddy Arnold worked. Since it was late and his work day was probably done, I chose to continue on to Old Town and my much-needed soak. It had been quite a day. I had participated in the 26.2-mile San Francisco Marathon, had entered a bike race, and covered a total of ninety-two miles.

My day finally ended when I booked a room in Old Sacramento directly beside the bike path that would take me to prison the following day.

The American River Bike Trail follows the shoreline of Folsom Lake. Riding through the wooded area was peaceful; the chaotic traffic and high temperatures of the previous day seemed far behind me.

I was startled by the shout of an oncoming biker.

"You're the biker riding across America," he said, and I recognized him as one of the two men I had met the day before. He lived in Davis, California, and had brought his daughter to Folsom for a youth event. On a whim, he also brought his bike along and was riding the trail while he waited for his daughter to conclude her activities. Now he asked me why I was biking across America, and we exchanged stories.

He was a doctor who had previously worked at Harvard Medical School. His wife was also a doctor; they had moved to Davis, where he had a pediatric practice and she joined the corporate world in medical research. After they had a child, he chose to quit his medical career and work from his home. This arrangement made it possible for him to care for his daughter and also follow his dream of becoming a woodworker; he now builds furniture in his little shop.

I so admired a man who was willing to quit a high-paying job to do what he enjoyed. Too many folks spend their lives dreaming about some faraway goal. So few actually have the courage to take steps toward that goal. I admired this doctor who became a woodworker. I did wonder if there might be a woodworker back in Amish Country who was dreaming about becoming a doctor.

At noon, I passed a sign announcing the entrance to Folsom Prison. A long, winding road led to the stern gray walls. This facility that Johnny Cash made famous houses 4,000 inmates. No tours are permitted; but I rode as close to the prison as possible, stopping at a guard house, where I entertained several guards with stories of my bike ride. One of them allowed me to stand in front of the prison wall while he snapped a photo.

In the space of two days, I had pedaled past three famous institutions of incarceration, San Quentin, just north of San Francisco, Alcatraz, and now Folsom. As I stood by Folsom's granite walls, I did not know that I would visit one more prison later in my journey, on a mission far different than sightseeing and a souvenir photo.

I stopped early that day. I wanted to rest and prepare for the big climb ahead of me. The next morning I would attack Carson Pass, crossing into Nevada as I crossed the mountain. It would be my highest climb yet, a peak 8,574 feet high. At a gas station in Placerville, I talked with a local who gave me directions for an alternate, supposedly easier route over the pass.

At five the next morning, I left Placerville by the light of the moon and began my slow uphill crawl. My route took me through the Eldorado National Forest, where stately pine trees crowded the narrow road. At a small outpost called Cooks Station, I stopped for a break.

I was leaving Cooks Station, ready to resume my ride, when I met a rider coming from the direction in which I was headed. He was a professor from Oakland, returning to his home on the coast. He told me he had been riding with a group that had left Oakland several days before. They intended to ride to Washington, D.C., on a trip they called "Bike for Peace." They weren't moving as fast as I was, and the professor thought there was a good chance I might catch up with them on the highway.

Included in this group was a former congresswoman from Atlanta, Cynthia McKinney. I'm a political junkie, and that name caught my attention. If you go to the left on the political spectrum and then continue even further left, you will find Cynthia McKinney. I'd often heard her speak on television, and I usually wanted to hurl my shoe at the screen in frustration. *If I ever get the chance to meet her, I'd certainly set her straight*, I'd think. But what were the chances of that ever happening?

Evening approached and I still had not conquered Carson Pass. Daylight was fading and I could not find a place to sleep. I felt panic clutching at me, but it was banished by relief when, in the faint light, I saw a sign for an inn. But disappointment set in when I discovered there was no room in this inn for me. There were no rooms at all, only a small dining establishment. I explained my dilemma to a server and asked about lodging nearby.

"There is nothing close by, but if you wait till I get off work in an hour, I'll take you and your bike to my hometown. It's forty miles on the other side of Carson Pass, and there are hotels there," she offered.

I told her about my cross-country bike ride and my own rule that I could not skip any sections.

"But no one will ever know you didn't bike those forty miles," she said.

"I'll know, and it would bother me forever if I didn't ride every mile of my trip."

"There's a fishing camp up the road several miles, up by Caples Lake. It has a small bunkhouse. You could try there." She knew the owner and tried to call the camp, to no avail. "Everything shuts down at dark up there, but you might be able to find the owner, if you want to ride up there and give it a try."

I regretted not purchasing a light to replace the one I had lost back in Washington. I did have a red flashing light on the back of my bike, so I was not totally invisible as I rode those miles through the near-darkness to Caples Lake. The entrance to the camp appeared, but a cable had been strung across the driveway. A CLOSED sign dangled from the cable, but I lifted my bike over it and hoped for the best.

A worker walking across the parking area directed me to the owner's cabin. When he answered my knock, I explained my dilemma and asked about accommodations.

"I do have a room in my bunkhouse that will cost you $105." I suspected that he was taking advantage of my desperation, but I was so weary from the day's uphill climb that I would not have turned down any price. It was a matter of supply and demand here, just as it had been in Forks, Washington.

I followed him to the bait and tackle shop where he took my money and handed me my room key. Posted on the wall were the room rates for his humble establishment. $70. Apparently there was a $35 upcharge for disturbing him after hours.

I struggled to maneuver my bike down a hallway littered with skis and dozens of boxes of solar panels. Then I lugged the bike up a dozen steps to my room on the second floor. The room was very small and did not have a bathroom. For that amenity, I would need to cross the hallway.

One detail about the room caused me some concern. Clothing that obviously belonged to a woman hung in one corner. The pillow on the bed seemed out of place, too; it was covered with designs of clouds. I surmised that perhaps a family member used this room occasionally and kept personal belongings here.

It had been the most brutal biking day of my trip. In fifteen hours, I had logged only sixty-six miles, sixty of which were uphill.

I was too exhausted to take a shower or a soak. I just needed to get some rest. At ten o'clock, I finally snapped off the light and slipped under the covers, laying my head to rest on a pillow of clouds.

I heard a rustling in the hallway. The approaching sound stopped at my doorway. A key was inserted into the lock. *Someone is obviously confused and has the wrong room*, I thought. But the key unlocked my door, and I could see a woman standing in the doorway.

"What are you doing in my bed?" the shocked woman asked.

"What are you doing in my room?" the equally shocked bike rider replied.

"This is my room," she said. "I paid for two nights. Didn't you see my clothes hanging there? And that's my cloud pillow your head is on." Admittedly, my head was in the clouds.

The woman insisted I find the owner and straighten out our predicament.

"No offense, but since I'm in bed and you're fully clothed, why don't you go see the owner and work it out?"

"No, you get out and fix this," she insisted. I had worked with enough women over the years to know when a battle is futile. This battle was lost the minute her key turned in the lock. I agreed to do the dirty work if she would kindly step out of the room and close the door so I could get into my clothes.

Back out into the darkness I went. I rapped on the cabin window and rousted the poor owner. He was amazed at my story of a woman sneaking into my room; then he slyly asked if the woman was attractive.

"I don't care if she's a Hollywood movie star. I just want to get some rest."

We stopped by the tackle store one more time to retrieve another key for the person evicted from the room. The owner apologized profusely to the lady for his error. Our conversation in the hallway drew two ladies from an adjoining room. They had heard the commotion and emerged to watch our little circus.

The situation was further defused by my silly humor. "I should have yelled 'Merry Christmas!' when you opened the door," I joked. After more formal introductions were made, the intruder and I discovered we were both Christians. Fortunately, we were both Christians with a sense of humor.

I moved my belongings down the hallway to another small room, one without ladies' garments and cloud pillows. Outside, the moon shone over Caples Lake and the waves lapped at the shore under my window and lulled me to sleep.

Just another day on the road across America.

CHAPTER 9

Middlegate Station

The night passed without further intrusions. As I pushed my bicycle past Room 1, I had an impulsive desire to jiggle my key in the lock. Let my new friend Danielle also experience the excitement of someone breaking into her room. But I restrained my ornery side and carried my ride down the flight of steps.

I breathed in the cool morning air and delighted in the scene before me. The moon was still visible over Caples Lake, and in the early morning light I was able to see what had been only shadowy forms in the dark the night before.

The occupants in Room 2 were also leaving. They had come into the hallway to watch the fray the previous evening, and now they officially introduced themselves. Debra had brought her daughter Margo out to these mountains to visit the site where she had scattered her own mother's ashes.

They also told me they had met Danielle the evening before I arrived. Mother and daughter had been dining at the same inn where I had sought lodging, the inn with no rooms. Danielle was there also, seated at another table and as yet a stranger to them. Striking up a conversation, they discovered not only that they were staying at the same lodge but also that they had more things in common. Danielle's family often visited the Caples area, and she had scattered her dad's ashes up in the mountains, too.

The cable was still stretched across the entrance, and I again lifted my bike over the obstruction and joined Route 88. Within an hour and much to my relief, I at last wheeled to the top of Mt. Carson, an elevation of 8,574 feet. Although I would reach much greater elevations later in Colorado, this was the highest mountain I had climbed since hiking through the Smokies two years earlier. I pulled over to the roadside and took in the awe-inspiring view. Below me lay the 600-acre Caples Lake, shimmering in the early morning light.

It was time to reap the reward of the previous day's uphill struggle. I would be leaving California and entering Nevada this morning. If all went well, I hoped to ride 113 miles to Fallon, Nevada. And nearly all of it would be coasting downhill.

Before leaving the mountaintop, I made one more adjustment. I had not yet had coffee that morning, but I did carry a foam coffee holder…between my two pairs of shorts. That foam accessory for early-morning get-up-and-go Joe was doing an admirable job of enhancing my riding pleasure. It worked wonders as I rotated it from cheek to cheek.

An amazing panorama of mountains and meadows unfurled before me that morning as I glided out of California. On Fredericksburg Road, I passed the Fredericksburg cemetery and was in Nevada. Ahead of me lay Carson City, and I already knew what challenge awaited me there. In Carson City I would meet up with US Route 50, known as the loneliest road in America.

How could it be any lonelier than those roads I had already traveled? I was finding this bike ride much lonelier than my hike on the Appalachian Trail. I was very much alone out here on the highway, and I sensed that intense loneliness was stalking me and was never far behind my whirling wheels. I'd been trying desperately to stay several bike lengths ahead of it. Could I outrun it on this desolate road that would take me across a hot barren desert and the entire state of Nevada?

On many of my downhill miles that day I relaxed, hunching over the handlebars, watching the landscape flow by. The temperature approached 100, but a slight breeze kept me from overheating. My front tire tube was not so fortunate. Back in Folsom, I had stopped at a bike shop and inflated my tires to the maximum capacity of 110 psi. Now the heat from the asphalt surface increased that pressure even further; and when I stopped for a rest break, I heard the front tube sigh. *Pssssst.* Apparently the pressures of life on the road were too much for it to handle.

Fortunately, the tube deflated while the bike and I were both at rest; but I was still about eighteen miles outside Fallon, alone in the hot desert. I unpacked my tool kit, including a tube of glue and tire patches. I had not had occasion to use the glue before and assumed I had a full tube of adhesive. Much to my surprise and dismay, the container was empty. Of all those tubes riding down the assembly line to be filled with product, I had purchased the one that declined filling. Fortunately, I carried an extra inner tube; and I inserted that instead of patching the blown one. With my little air pump, I inflated the tire to half capacity and cautiously continued on to Fallon.

At a service station in Fallon, I pressurized my tire short of capacity and went in search of a room. Later, a trip to Wal-Mart replaced my empty tube of adhesive with a full one. I also purchased a new headlight to replace the one I'd lost just before crossing into Oregon, and I finally bought a pair of sunglasses. I'd not felt a need for them before, but who crosses a desert without eye protection?

The next morning I began a new ritual. Remembering how Bobby White laid his hands over his door frame and blessed it each time he passed through, I determined to do the same with my wheels. The gentle laying on of hands was accompanied by a little ditty I had composed:

Keep my wheels going round and round,
keep my bicycle on the ground,

83

keep my tires full of air,
bless and keep me everywhere.

Perhaps not up to Nashville standards. Certainly not destined to be flashed on any church wall during praise service.

My goal for that day was a little outpost called Middlegate Station, fifty miles out in the desert. Ahead of me on Route 50 there were many stretches where there was no service of any kind for up to eighty miles. I decided to stop for the night at Middlegate and chart out the remainder of my ride with whatever information I could acquire there.

I rode through miles and miles of nothing. Salt beds covered the desert floor with crusty layers of white crystals. Sand dunes rolled on for miles, visible at great distances. Miles were difficult to judge. The curve in the road that I thought was just a mile ahead turned out to be ten miles away. The land was barren, with only sparse sagebrush. And it was hot.

It was a solitary ride through the empty desert, and I could feel the loneliness creeping closer. I did see signs of mining in the area, and occasionally a big truck roared past me. Military aircraft sometimes screamed overhead. The US Navy uses this area as a training ground for pilots in the Top Gun program. They actually drop bombs to the desert floor during training. Later I would joke to one of the workers at Middlegate Station that the practice bombings actually improved the landscape.

If the desert was foreign terrain for me, Middlegate Station was as close as possible to being on another planet. Or, rather, it was in another century. Middlegate was a stagecoach stop in the 1800s. The Pony Express stopped here to change horses. Time had also stopped in this little cluster of buildings and never moved on. Very little has changed since the last stagecoach clattered up to the station. A dilapidated old carriage was parked outside, and a welcoming sign on the front wall read,

WELCOME TO MIDDLEGATE
THE MIDDLE OF NOWHERE
ELEVATION 4600 FEET
POPULATION 18

The "18" had been crossed out and a "17" written beside it. Middlegate Station is slowly decreasing in population and will probably soon be covered over by shifting sand dunes. Of course, a misdirected bomb from its nearby neighbor, Uncle Sam, could also cause some changes.

A string of mobile homes had been cobbled together end-for-end and given a cheap façade, creating lodging accommodations. The reasonable cost of a room at the makeshift motel—only $30— more than made up for the previous rip-offs I'd suffered. The first order of business was a shower to wash off the hot desert sticking to my body. Refreshed in spirit, I set out to explore the compound.

I had dropped down a rabbit hole into another realm. Several weather-beaten outbuildings dotted the area and rusty vehicles and campers sagged into the sand. Horses in the corral and dogs drifting around the buildings almost doubled the population. Middlegate Station itself was a ramshackle, tin-roofed building housing a bar and small restaurant. Outside, an old gas pump and a propane tank still offered services, right next to an ancient wooden telephone booth. Inside Middlegate Station was The Henhouse Grill, just an open grill in the corner of the bar; but, oh, what good food came from that crowded corner!

Should I live to be 100, I doubt I will ever meet so many eccentric characters in one place as I did during my two days at Middlegate.

While waiting for my lunch, I struck up conversation with Russell, the bartender and waiter. Russell was a lanky, unassuming character in blue jeans and a big hat, glasses and a graying beard. My first thought was that he was probably an out-of-luck drifter that had taken up residence here and worked for food and board. But I discovered he was a biologist who had moved here eighteen years before to study the desert. At the time, this Great Basin desert through which I was riding was the only desert in the world he had not studied. He spent one nine-month period living in a tent near a spring in the desert, observing the longhorn sheep and mountain lions. At night, wild mustangs came to the spring to drink. In the morning when it turned cold, he'd make a fire out of the brittle undergrowth of rabbitbrush.

Sensing a connection with this man who obviously loved nature, I asked if he ever read Edward Abbey, a Western nature writer who was known as Cactus Ed, as much for his prickly demeanor and his witted barbs as for his writings about the actual cactus in his beloved desert. I thought Russell even looked something like Edward Abbey.

At the mention of Abbey's name, a faraway look came into Russell's eyes, and I saw a tear slide down his cheek. "You really got me there, young man," he said. "In my eighteen years here, you're the first person to mention Ed Abbey. My wife and I used to read his work to each other when we were studying in Nicaragua." Earlier, Russell had spoken fondly of the years with his wife in Central America, and I knew his wife was no longer with him. Not having enough sense to stop prying, I asked if recalling those good memories had brought the tears.

"Oh, no, it's not that," he said. "It's the desert. The desert." He repeated the word sadly. "It's what they are doing to the desert. They're destroying it. They're even building golf courses out there in the desert."

My food arrived and Russell was busy with other customers. I started conversation with Kathy, who was the wife of the owner and ruled the roost at the Henhouse Grill.

"How did you end up out here in the desert?"

"You have to be unusual to survive out here," she told me, "and we all have our own stories. Some people are here, hiding from whatever or whoever is chasing them. Some of us actually enjoy this place. I worked for many years in Lake Tahoe, and the stresses of an upper management job drove me out here."

Another character joined me at the counter. Kathy introduced me to Sleeping Bag Bill, a nephew of the owner of Middlegate Station. His uncle had given him room and board in exchange for work when Bill had been laid off at the local cat litter mine. Several miles out in the desert, an operation was mining zeolite, the active ingredient in cat litter.

But Bill had a drinking problem and a penchant for doing crazy things. Parked out in front of the building was an R100RT BMW motorcycle. This was Bill's ride. The bike had no windshield, and so he placed a sleeping bag between his handlebars to divert the wind. The sleeping bag was also convenient for those times he had imbibed too much and was not able to find his way home. Thus, his nickname.

In front of Middlegate Station was a long stretch of road where Bill liked to show off by riding down the road while standing on his seat and pretending to be surfing. After too much alcohol, he did this foolish trick without the benefit of clothing. That was excessive even for Middlegate standards, and his cycle was grounded.

Sleeping Bag Bill had returned from Vietnam hooked on heroin but had managed to kick that habit. He had, however, traded that bad life choice for another. Now he was using marijuana.

"I am trying to quit that, too," he told me. But recently he had run afoul of the law because of his habit. "My brother called and said my mom was dying. He asked me to bring a joint to smoke after mom died." I looked at Bill with surprise and he shrugged. "Hey, that's just the way we are."

His brother picked up Bill and they headed for California, but they were pulled over for a speeding violation. While the officer was at the window, Bill had an idea. He always carried a harmonica in his pocket. Why not entertain the law with some music? Sadly, the little joint intended for the funeral popped out with the harmonica, and he was busted. He now had a court date to contend with.

Several other folks joined us at the counter. Their introductions included the information that they were riding bicycles coast to coast, on a trip called Bike for Peace. That sounded familiar. While I was slowly climbing Carson Pass, the biking professor had told me about these cyclists.

"Are you the group Cynthia McKinney is riding with?" I inquired. It was indeed the same group, and we discussed their plans for crossing Nevada. They had six riders and a support vehicle. Their plan was to cross the desert by riding in the cool of night instead of the heat of day. The vehicle would follow them, carrying extra water and food.

"We're going to take a rest day here tomorrow, then we'll start across Nevada. You're welcome to join us if you'd like."

Several thoughts flashed through my mind. Another whole day here would certainly be interesting. I was meeting some eccentric characters, and my trip was all about meeting the people of America. And they had a support vehicle. And this might be my chance to meet Cynthia McKinney. And I would not be alone on the loneliest road in America. The decision was easy. I would ride with them across the desert.

I dubbed the group "the Peace Train" and became the seventh member. As more riders trickled in, I was introduced to the passengers on my night train to Utah. Our group had two Universalists, folks who believe in numerous gods. We had one atheist, who believed in no god; one agnostic, who didn't know what to believe; one congresswoman; one gay lady; and one Christian (yours truly). God does work in mysterious ways.

Later, back in my small room in the makeshift motel, I felt the entire trailer shaking. An earthquake perhaps? I investigated. Attached to the outside wall was an open deck with a washer and dryer where Bill was now doing laundry. The dryer was unbalanced and dancing a jig, causing the entire deck and my walls to shudder.

As I went out on the deck, I saw a small fluffy dog in a pickup. The little critter sat on the front seat and growled at me. Bill explained that a "sort-of" girlfriend had asked Bill to watch the dog for two weeks. Two months went by, and the sort-of girlfriend had never returned. The night before, Bill had again drunk too much and had forgotten to let the little dog out of the pickup. Now the dog refused to leave the truck at all.

Bill told me more about his situation.

"After being laid off from the cat litter plant, I had no money and nowhere to go. There's nothing to do out here but drink, so that's what I do. I do just enough work to buy my alcohol."

"What about family?" I asked.

"Mom and Dad are both gone. So are my grandparents. I was just a kid, at my grandparents' house one day. They were both in their eighties, and Grandmother was starting with Alzheimer's. That day my grandfather had a ladder out to climb up on the roof. When he stepped down from the ladder, he accidentally stepped on Grandmother's petunia patch. She got real angry and yelled at Gramps to get out of the petunia patch. He gave a dismissive kick at a petunia plant, and that pushed Grandma over the edge. She went inside the house and returned with a .44 pistol and shot Gramps dead on the spot. She just looked at me and said, 'I've wanted to do that for a long time.' Grandma went to jail and died soon after. I guess after awhile, enough is enough," said Bill.

I questioned the accuracy of Bill's stories, but decided to believe him. I realized just how blessed I was and silently thanked God for placing me in a Christian home.

As I walked across the parking lot to my room that evening, I was granted my wish. Cynthia McKinney and I met. She was the African-American congresswoman from Georgia whose liberal views and opinions had caused me such consternation; I was the politically conservative Mennonite from Holmes County. And in the twilight, we had a conversation that can only be described as divine.

Cynthia's father had just passed away and she had also recently lost her favorite aunt after a botched surgery. This bike trip was not just a ride for peace for her, but a healing journey much like my Appalachian hike had been for me. We discussed loss and the pain of those left behind. I knew immediately that this was a

God-ordained meeting. This was one of the folks God had in mind when He sent me out on this ride.

We discussed politics; Cynthia had been the Green Party candidate for president in the 2008 election and was now mulling over her political options. For the following week, she was never far from her cell phone, taking calls from her advisors. She good-naturedly accepted my offer to become her newest political advisor, and I informed her with a grin that she needed to move just a smidgeon to the right.

"Cynthia, there is so much hatred in Washington, D.C. Isn't it time to put aside all those divisions on Capitol Hill? Can't you all start speaking out of love for one another instead?"

"Hate sells," she informed me. "Hate wins elections."

"Hate may sell for a season, but love will eventually conquer all. God has you out here in the desert for a reason. You could be the person who starts the change in Washington."

We hugged each other and agreed to continue our conversation throughout the week.

During the night, I awoke to discover the door to my room was hanging wide open. A shift of the mobile home room had un-latched the door. I stepped outside and was amazed by the brilliant stars twinkling in the desert sky. Those stars would be the canopy over my night riding for the next week.

Morning came, and I needed coffee. Russell was again behind the counter and our conversation continued. Russell is an atheist and believes that there is no God. He also believes the world will end on December 21, 2012. Apparently, this day is the end of the Mayan calendar and time will cease to exist.

"Well, Russell, if you are correct and the world does end on December 21, 2012, that will also be the day you'll no longer be an atheist." Russell just grinned at my reference to meeting God on that date. He laughed when I asked if I could bill my breakfast and pay for it December 22, 2012.

Sleeping Bag Bill again joined us with his wisdom. He grinned toward Russell and informed me that he could always tell if a person was a good server by looking at the back part of the body. If a server was wearing a tool belt with tools dangling from it (an accessory Russell was indeed wearing), the server probably didn't belong behind a counter. "A good server should have ample hips," declared Bill. I had been in the restaurant business twenty-five years and had hired hundreds of servers; now, only after I retire, do I finally discover the secret.

Throughout the day, Middlegate Station was the stopping point for other weary travelers. On the front porch, I met seventy-six-year-old Passin' Through. He drove a pickup truck pulling a small Airstream trailer.

"I'm Don, but I'm known as 'Passin' Through'."

"Where are you headed?"

"Oh, just down the road." That was the standard reply for him. His *down the road* meant about thirty-five miles a day. He'd pull off the road and spend the night wherever pleased him.

Red scars reached across his forehead. Several weeks before, while he was parked at an area beside the highway, a golden eagle had mistaken his white hair for a rabbit and had landed on his head, scratching those furrows across his face. Passin' Through ended up at the hospital and was sutured up.

Tears filled his eyes as he explained that after forty-four years of marriage his wife informed him she wanted a divorce. He had worked as an airline pilot flying 737s and had flown the F-105 Thunderbird in air shows. Retired at last and looking forward to traveling with his spouse, she instead wanted out and had left him. Their home and possessions were sold; and in the end, he was also alienated from his children and grandchildren.

"My home was in Denver, but I've been on the road now for six years. The divorce tore my family apart, and no one really knows the truth about what happened. My children don't want to see me. My grandson is an all-state football player, and sometimes I drive past the stadium and wish I could see him play. Now home is wherever I stop for the night. I'm happiest when I see Denver in my rearview mirror; then I know my family troubles are behind me."

Our conversation was interrupted by a commotion in the parking lot. A white van careened to a dusty stop and all forms of humanity crawled out. A group of gypsy girls had arrived. Bizarre haircuts topped bodies decorated with all manner of piercings and tattoos. I picked out the girl with the most outlandish appearance and asked her where they were headed.

They had no destination, simply drifting from one part of the country to another, playing their guitars at places they stopped, depending on donations to pay for food and gas. They'd pick up anyone along the way who needed a ride. Everyone who hitched a ride in the van autographed the interior walls before parting with their company. She invited me to check out the van. The inside walls were completely covered with names and messages. Many of the notes were quite vulgar. A bumper sticker on the side of the van announced, THE PARTY IN HELL HAS BEEN CANCELLED DUE TO THE FIRE. Perhaps that would be humorous if it were not so serious. There's a whole generation of kids out in the world who think hell is a joke. Sadly, many moms and dads have failed their kids and the children are wandering out there on life's highways.

Back on the porch at Middlegate Station, I asked the pierced and tattooed one where home was and if she missed it. She was silent for several moments.

"Mom and Dad got divorced and I hated them both. I couldn't even talk to my mom until just recently. But, yeah, I do miss her, and I often wish I could go home."

A loud boom thundered from the other side of the building. Then came more explosions. Sleeping Bag Bill had filled several plastic two-liter bottles with water and baking soda. As the pressure expanded the containers, Bill took his pistol and shot them. His targets were right next to the old gas pump. Why wait for Uncle Sam to drop bombs on Middlegate Station, when Sleeping Bag Bill can blow up the place all by himself?

I had one more place to visit. Several folks had talked about a shoe tree down the road. They'd taken me to the parking lot and pointed out a tree far in the distance. Legend says that a young bride and groom driving down Route 50 on their wedding night had an argument and the groom stopped at that tree and kicked his wife out. He left her under the big cottonwood to cool off and he drove to Middlegate Station for a drink. When he returned and she was still angry, he threw a pair of her shoes up in the tree and went back to the bar for another drink. The third time he came back to his bride, she had calmed down; but the shoes were stuck up in the tree and they could not retrieve them. The newlyweds left the shoes hanging there, and later other folks added shoes of their own. Now the cottonwood had hundreds of pairs of shoes hanging from its branches and several thousand more scattered around its base.

"It's only a mile down the road," the storytellers had said. Like everything else in the desert, it was farther than it looked. I visited the tree, but pedaled a six-mile round trip.

Coming back to Grand Central Station, I found the place hopping. The gypsy girls were banging away on guitars and wailing and howling like banshees while folks were eating supper at the counter. I would have gladly donated money to stop the howling if I had wanted to stay in the building, but I needed to get some rest. The night train would be departing the station at midnight.

In that barren desert, I watched the tumbleweed skid along highways and over the sand. Separated from their roots, the brown and dead-looking clumps of weeds are blown along, scattered in whatever direction the wind takes them. And I'd think of the many people I met who were also drifting—vagabond lives tumbling along, separated from their roots, human tumbleweed.

All of us wanderers seek a place called *Home,* a place of refuge, a place where it is safe to be ourselves and still be loved. Some search all their lives and never quite find it. I felt like I was tumbling across this country, too, on a solitary journey, far from home. But I wasn't a drifter or a vagabond; I tumbled along, firmly anchored to God.

CHAPTER 10

The Peace Train

I was awakened at midnight by shuffling on the wooden porch outside my door. The Peace Train was preparing for departure. Six of us would be riding; Cynthia would follow several hours later in the car with extra water and snacks.

Our tires crunched over the gravel parking lot as we left the sleeping Middlegate Station. Rarely in life does a person hear so many diverse stories as I had during my short stay here. Had I stayed several more days, I believe I would have enough material to write an entire book. I briefly entertained the thought of returning someday to that speck in the desert just for the entertainment.

The night air was cool and I had slipped on my rain jacket. I had two new pieces of equipment. Back in Fallon, I had purchased a foam seat cover for my bike seat. I now had a layer of foam on the bike seat and another layer of foam riding between my two pairs of biker shorts. That foam cup holder was working splendidly. I had also purchased a light to replace the one lost back in Washington State. It was a lamp with straps attached, intended to be used as a headlamp. I wrapped the straps around the handlebars and that arrangement worked quite well, allowing me to grasp the lamp and shine it in any direction I wished.

The stars were blazing across the desert sky as I pedaled past the shoe tree with hundreds of shoes dangling eerily from its branches. Off in the distance, unusual lights glowed on the hillsides and the pungent aroma of burning sagebrush wafted across our path. A brush fire raged unchecked; it had been burning for several days and already had scorched several thousand acres. Over the past two days, firefighters had been using Middlegate as a base as they attempted to keep the fire under control.

We spent most of the night climbing, first over New Pass Summit at 6,348 feet and then Mt. Airy Summit at 6,679 feet. Our destination was the town of Austin, halfway up a third mountain called Austin Pass.

The members of the Peace Train were all considerably younger than I and were stronger riders, but my stubbornness and pride kept me with the group most of the night. At last, though, I had to admit that the smart plan would be to ride at my own pace and get there whenever I got there. This meant riding alone in the dark, deserted desert.

The miles rolled by and the darkness of night slowly faded away. Out over the Toiyabe Mountain Range, a faint glow emanated. Soon a bright red sliver of sun emerged and the desert floor was bathed in early morning light. I stopped and soaked up the warm sunbeams that rejuvenated my spirit.

At eight in the morning, I arrived in Austin. This had been a stop for the Pony Express, a mail delivery system covering 1,800 miles from St. Joseph, Missouri, to Sacramento, California. The qualifications for being hired as a rider were to be young, skinny, and wiry. The dangers were great and the chances were high that a rider might be killed, so the company preferred to hire orphans. The story in Austin was that a Pony Express horse galloped through town one day and kicked over a rock, exposing a vein of silver. Austin soon became a silver-mining town and by 1863 had a population of over 10,000 people.

It appeared that nothing as exciting as a horse galloping through town happens here nowadays. The population has dwindled to about 300, and I walked the length of the town and spied only one other person roaming about.

After checking into my room at the Lincoln Motel, I crossed the street to the café where the rest of the group had gathered for breakfast. I placed my order and went in search of a bathroom. But in my fatigued state, I removed the outer pair of bike shorts and neglected to first remove my foam coffee cup holder. Comfort Joe took this opportunity to make its escape, but met an untimely demise. The poor mug holder had indeed won its freedom, but was then doing the backstroke in the toilet bowl. Very gingerly, I caught it between thumb and forefinger and dropped it into the trash container. It had served me well, but now I would once again browse my roadside department store for comfort. Since I would be riding in darkness the next few nights, there was little chance I'd find a replacement soon.

I had pushed hard to ride the seventy miles to Austin. The stretch from Austin to my next stop, Eureka, was another seventy miles with no services.

That night, I decided to depart an hour before the rest of the group. At midnight, I climbed the long hill out of town, under a waning crescent moon that glowed in the star-speckled sky. Rounding Austin Peak, I started a steep, three-mile downhill. My lamp lit the way as I careened down the highway. Then another steep uphill over Bob Scott Summit and another extended downhill. The miles were flowing by swiftly, with not a car in sight. Except for the yipping of coyotes, the only sounds were the hum of my bike tires and the whirring of the chain.

Then far ahead a speck of light glowed. Many miles later, I passed a farmhouse with a pole light casting its pale yellow hue over the quiet farmhouse and yard. The scene tugged at my heart. This was a home. Not mine, of course. But to someone, that little area lit by a yellow circle in the desert night represented home. I felt very alone, far from comfort and safety. I pedaled harder and faster, feeling the loneliness creeping ever closer.

At three o'clock, several specks of light bobbed in the darkness behind me. The Peace Train was slowly gaining on me. Just knowing they were nearby gave comfort and staved off the palpable loneliness stalking me.

Back in Ohio, Leonard Hartmann was following my journey in *The Budget,* a newspaper widely read in the Amish community. *The Budget* printed weekly updates on my journey, and Leonard realized I would be passing through Eureka, Nevada, where his daughter and son-in-law lived. Leonard had emailed the Martins' phone number to me in case I needed a place to stay.

I checked into a motel in downtown Eureka and walked across the street to the Owl Café for a hearty breakfast. After that, I planned to sleep the Sunday away.

While I waited for my food to arrive, a group of motorcycle riders roared up to the café. This was not a church group out on a day trip. These riders were members of Hell's Angels, the most feared motorcycle club in America. A group of fifteen rough-looking men, leather jackets emblazoned with club regalia, swaggered in and seated themselves. A hush fell over the other tables.

These were not people to be messed with. The Hell's Angels have been involved in murders and are accused of many criminal activities. They never lock their clubhouses and their bikes are never disturbed. Folks intent on mischief against this gang know retribution will be swift and sure. Everyone knows that stealing from a member of the club may result in an untimely demise.

Terrorists operate in the same way. Their power lies in threats and certainty of retaliation. Newspapers will not print anything against a beloved prophet, fearing reprisal. People and countries bow to demands, afraid of the consequences of resistance.

Although I oppose everything both groups stand for, they do prove one thing: Punishment is effective if it is enforced consistently and unfailingly. It is certainly true that our nation is a weaker nation because our punishment for wrongdoing is inconsistent.

Finished with breakfast, I got up to leave and was tempted to ask one of the riders if bicyclists could join their gang; but better judgment kept me walking and pinched my lips.

I had noticed that every now and then a member would leave the rowdy group and step outside the restaurant. As I left, I passed one gang member outside, apparently on the phone with his wife. These men were coming outside to call wives and girlfriends. While inside with the gang, everyone was loud and boisterous. Now I overheard one telling his wife he would be home soon and that he loved and missed her. Macho with the gang; but when removed from the group, he became a teddy bear.

On the sidewalks of Eureka, in front of a row of Harley motorcycles, I again was reminded that the solution to the ills of our society is love. Whether in the halls of congress or in our homes and churches, only love can bring us together.

Back in my room, I decided to call the Martins to let them know I was in town. Cervin and Jean Martin and their family had just returned from church and were sitting down to their noon meal. I hesitated for two seconds before accepting an invitation to join them. Several minutes later I was picked up by Mr. Martin and enjoyed a great home-cooked meal. It was my second meal in two hours. The next night's ride to Ely would be a difficult seventy-eight miles, but I would ride loaded with calories.

At one in the morning, I pedaled through a deserted Eureka. Stars again sparkled brilliantly overhead. Off in the distance, the coyotes yipped night messages across the plains. Crickets serenaded me as I passed. Many times I paused to rest and gaze upward at the vast heavens. Millions of stars and constellations formed patterns across the night sky. It was as if God Himself had written a message of love to me. Occasionally a meteor blazed across the heavens, a veritable exclamation mark to the starry message.

It was a night of four big uphills followed by exhilarating downhill charges through the darkness. In between the mountains lay vast stretches of open desert. Several times during the night a pinprick of light would appear far off in the distance. Ten minutes later, the single pinprick would slowly turn into two growing orbs of light; and eventually a car or truck would pass me.

Just before dawn, the desert turns cold. Even wearing my rain jacket and gloves, I shivered until the welcome sun peeked over the horizon.

Morning brought visitors out of the sagebrush. Rattlesnakes slithered onto the highway, seeking the warmth held in the pavement. Many had met a fatal end when introduced to the Michelin Man and Mr. Goodyear. Even dead, those snakes gave me a start whenever I happened upon one.

It was a difficult night of climbs, and with great relief I at last pulled myself over Robinson Summit. I was at an elevation of 7,588 feet and had fifteen downhill miles into Ely. What should have been a swift flight into town was complicated by strong air currents heading west. I was heading east. For the next fifteen miles, I wrangled with the headwind.

The Peace Train had long ago passed me, and twice Cynthia drove out from Ely to check on my progress. She insisted that I get in the car and let her drive me into town. I just as insistently turned down her offer. But I'm convinced that having to pedal on a downhill slope is not what God intended bicycling to be.

Located in White Pine County, Ely was another stagecoach stop and Pony Express station. Ely was a late arrival to the mining scene. In 1906 copper was discovered, the railroad came to town, and Ely boomed. Later in the twentieth century, though, copper prices dropped and mines were closed. There are still six open pits gouged out of the desert, the largest of which is 1,000 feet deep, one mile wide, and two miles long.

My stop was the Hotel Nevada and Gambling Hall in downtown Ely. In 1929, this hotel opened and claimed the title of the tallest building in the state; it was all of six stories tall. Once a stop for many public figures and Hollywood stars, the hotel may have been an attractive and impressive place in 1929, but it has lost its luster. Very little has changed over the past eighty years. My room was $40, a bargain. Several rows of slot machines on the main floor offered diversion to those wishing to pay extra for their stay.

The old cast iron tub, sitting atop curved legs, cradled me in hot water and my aches and pains melted away. It had been a hard, eighty-mile ride, made even more difficult by the absence of my foam padding.

Later, I strolled through the streets of Ely, virtually alone. Ely still has a population of around 4,000. After the copper mines were abandoned, gold was discovered; now a large mining operation sifts through the copper trailings in search of the precious metal. The area encompassing Ely and nearby Ruth is still the largest producer of gold in the state, but the town's streets and buildings are faded and neglected. It was a story I saw repeated again and again in Nevada. Robust mining centers, previously hubs of wealth and commerce, now are veritable ghost towns.

The next day's ride would take our group to a little town just shy of the Utah border. I left a sleeping Ely at one in the morning. For several hours I rode in silence as the lights of the town receded into the darkness behind me. It was always comforting knowing the Peace Train was somewhere behind me. Around three o'clock, they caught up with me and then, one by one, disappeared into the night ahead.

Two large mountain climbs and one vast valley lay between me and Baker. Five miles west of Baker, I passed the entrance to the Great Basin National Park. I would leave Route 50 here. The lonely highway across the Nevada desert had lived up to its reputation.

A secondary highway, Route 487, took me into the town of Baker. Several times in the early morning I heard water rushing out from the desert. Baker has the good fortune of sitting atop a huge water reservoir. This good fortune has also brought bad fortune: The small settlement of Baker is at war. The enemy lies 250 miles farther south.

Las Vegas is the fastest growing city in America. Someone had the foresight to build a huge city with its mega resorts in a desert. Deserts are generally dry areas. It would not seem to be the smartest place to pursue building a city. Nevertheless, they did. Las Vegas is running out of water and is looking for other aquifers to suck dry. A $2 billion pipeline from Baker to Las Vegas is on the drawing board and is now a hot issue for the locals. Las Vegas wants to funnel sixteen billion gallons of water a year from Baker's water table.

This water war is now being waged between the two towns; in the future, access to water has the potential to become a volatile political issue. Look out, Great Lakes! They may be coming for you next.

At eight the next morning, we arrived in Baker to an unwelcome reception. The lady running the Silver Jack Inn would not allow us to check in. This was the first time during our night rides that we encountered this restriction. The lady was rigid and unbending. One by one, our group attempted to negotiate with the obstinate proprietor. "I need to cook breakfast for my guests. Then I need to clean rooms. The earliest you can check in is two o'clock, like the sign says."

I thought perhaps my charm might convince the stubborn lady to take pity on us tired bikers. After all, hadn't I been an intense student of the female psyche during all those years of negotiating the minefield of workplace femininity? I invited my new friend Cynthia McKinney along to observe my tactics of persuasion and to perhaps learn a few things herself.

Apparently, I hadn't learned enough. I struck out against the cantankerous lady. My charm never stood a chance against her pitiless, cold heart. I proceeded to lecture her on the merits of hospitality, declaring she was the most stubborn, bullheaded, headstrong person I had ever met and this was no way to run a business. I then suggested she have a pleasant day and I bid her adieu. Yes, I did regret my attitude later and asked God to forgive me. I may have botched an appointment He had planned for me.

All this time, Cynthia stood nearby, observing my futile attempts at persuasion. But she did not follow me when I left the small lobby and joined the rest of the group outside. We sat and pondered our dilemma. But still no Cynthia appeared. Ten minutes passed, and she finally emerged from the front door with a smile and keys to our rooms.

I was astounded and shocked.

"Cynthia, how…what…what did you do?"

With a sly grin she replied, "Not much, really. I just stood there by the register and didn't say much. Our grumpy lady asked what I was still doing there, and I told her I would stand there until she let us check in." The lady realized Cynthia really meant to stand there in front of her desk as long as was necessary.

Both Grumpy Lady and I had met someone more stubborn than both of us. A powerful lesson soaked through my fatigued brain. Actions speak louder than words. While I had railed against the poor service and unfriendly attitude, Cynthia had silently taken a stand. No yelling, just persistence, and a refusal to give up and go away had saved the day. How I admired Cynthia's determination that morning.

That day, Cynthia and I spoke at length about the irony of our meeting, two people whose views were so different, thrown together in the desert, becoming friends. I spoke of God's love and again voiced my belief that God had a role for her to play in bringing civility back to government. Love triumphs over all. We talked of love, hate, politics, grief, healing, and our personal beliefs. And I reminded her that I would be available as a campaign advisor should she decide to run for office again.

At ten that evening, I was again pedaling east. No longer on the official loneliest road, I nevertheless was starting an eighty-five-mile stretch with no services.

In just a few short miles, I reached a welcoming sign. WELCOME TO UTAH, said the sign, brightly lit against the dark night. It was a toll sign of sorts, since it cost me one hour of time when I crossed over the Utah line. That hour had been gifted to me previously while flying over Utah on my way to Seattle. I gladly returned it, since it meant being one time zone closer to home.

The highway I followed now changed to Utah Route 21. This was the road I would pedal all night to Milford, Utah.

It appeared that I would be caught in a thunderstorm. Lights flashed in the distance. But, curiously, there was no thunder. I was witnessing the amazing phenomenon called the northern lights. For hours, brilliant flares lit the horizon. It was the Fourth of July, witnessed from a bicycle seat.

Several hours passed before the Peace Train caught up with me. Most of the group passed me and disappeared, but Annie and I rode side by side for an hour, engrossed in conversation. I really knew little about my fellow bikers; I was only a hobo on this train. On the road to Milford, in the darkness of night, Annie gave me more insight into the group.

She herself had been raised in a large Catholic family and had chosen a lifestyle that her family opposed. I spoke about God's love for her and the saving grace of Jesus.

There were two men in their twenties in the group; one absolutely knew God didn't exist and the other thought it might be possible there was a God, but he didn't really care if God existed or not. I was baffled. How could one view those northern lights flaring in the distance and not believe in a higher power?

The two group leaders were both Unitarian Universalists. This is perhaps the most liberal church in America. You don't have to believe in God, or you can believe in as many gods as you wish. Many members worship many different gods. I wondered if they would need appointments to be judged by all the different gods on judgment day. The church also doesn't believe in hell, so perhaps that judgment issue would be moot. I am happy to know that one day I will be judged by only one God, the God who is in control of the northern lights, who created everything I passed through, and who claimed me as His son.

Not a single car had passed us; and since Annie was with me, I took a break, stretched out on the warm road surface, and allowed myself a short nap. It would be nine hours that night before any vehicle appeared on Utah Route 21.

The early glint of dawn and I arrived on Frisco Summit at the same time. Although fatigued to the bone, I paused to take in the scene. Empty plains stretched out below me. Those plains rolled into more mountain ranges with undulating waves of peaks and slopes beyond. The views were majestic, but I wondered how many more climbs there were for these legs, these lungs, and that one part of my anatomy that was never comfortable…

Slowly I mounted my bike and pushed off the mountaintop for the fifteen-mile downhill ride to Milford, Utah, our stop for that day.

There would be one more night ride, from Milford to Cedar City, Utah. It would only be a fifty-seven-mile stretch, so the Peace Train would not leave until four in the morning. At three-thirty, the clouds hid the moon as I pedaled out of Milford toward the next little town, Minersville, fifteen miles away. We would be leaving Route 21 in Minersville; so I had been careful to get proper directions for our planned route.

At five o'clock, I arrived in Minersville. I wanted to find the new route, but it was still dark and I was soon totally lost. What a relief to finally see the lights of the Peace Train bobbing along the dark highway. They joined me in my confusion. We meandered the streets, unable to find Route 130 which would lead us over the last mountain and into Cedar City. One member of the group realized he had a GPS on his phone; and by the miracle of modern technology, we finally escaped Minersville and headed toward Cedar City.

A long stretch upward took us to a mountaintop. From there we could see our destination thirty miles away, a city lying in a long valley ringed with mountains. Interstate 15 runs through Cedar City, and in the distance, I could see the bridge I would cross over the interstate.

Little yellow sunflowers along the roadside brightened the journey. These little buttons of golden joy were also useful in determining wind direction, bending before the winds sweeping through the mountains. Along the last five miles to Cedar City, the pretty flowers bowed low in my direction as a strong headwind tried to blow me back to Nevada.

I was riding deep into Mormon country. One thing Mormons have in common with my Amish friends back home is meticulously manicured properties. Homes had lush green lawns, with sprinklers flowing freely. Fields were also irrigated and newly cut hay lay ready for baling. Any areas that were not irrigated were arid and brown. I guessed that Cedar City had decided to use their own water before Las Vegas could send a pipeline in their direction.

I crossed the bridge over Interstate 15 and found Main Street, running through downtown Cedar City. The Peace Train had booked small cabins at a nearby KOA Campground. It was time for me to separate from this group and strike out on my own again. Their company as I crossed the desert had been an answer to prayer; but now I was headed into the unknown, once again alone.

After a sad good-bye to my friend Cynthia, I headed down Main Street and rewarded myself with a night at a lovely Best Western Hotel. I checked in at ten in the morning, and no rooms were cleaned. Seeing how tired I was, the manager helped to clean a room for me. I appreciated the kindness, even more so since I had experienced the lack of compassion from that lady in Baker.

I did laundry and again scrounged through my panniers and sent home everything I thought was not absolutely essential. I managed to lighten my load by another five pounds.

There was one more task, finding a replacement for that foam coffee insulator that had done a high dive. At a supermarket down the street, I once again prowled the aisles, scouring the shelves for potential comfort. In the end, I chose a pack of Dr. Scholl's® shoe inserts. This seemed the perfect solution. Two size 11s covering each cheek might work wonders down yonder.

With that problem solved, there was only one fitting way to celebrate the conclusion of my night rides across the desert. Next door, a steakhouse promised juicy steaks. I accepted the invitation. A good, thick slab of beef was just the antidote for the weariness of the road.

I had been on that bicycle seat for twenty-seven days. Tomorrow was still a mystery; only God knew what waited for me down the road. But for tonight, all was well with my world.

CHAPTER 11

Night in Utah Hell

I pushed my bike out into the darkness on Main Street. It was four o'clock in the morning. A shadowy figure loomed up out of the darkness, giving me a brief moment of alarm before I realized it was a life-sized statue. Several prominent citizens of the area had been immortalized in bronze and stood along the sidewalk, watching silently as I pedaled down the empty street.

My size 11 Dr. Scholl's followed behind, doing an admirable job as my rear guard. Tucked securely in place between the two pairs of biking shorts, they did indeed seem custom fit for the pain relief I needed.

I searched for Center Street, where Route 14 headed east toward what would be my hardest climb thus far. The top of Black Mountain rises to an elevation of 10,375 feet, and for days I had been dreading this stretch of road. I'd be climbing upward for almost twenty-six miles, headed toward Cedar Breaks National Monument. I told myself it was just a matter of moving forward and tackling what lay ahead. Often in life we encounter problems the size of mountains and we anticipate great difficulty; but once we tackle those obstacles, we realize they are not insurmountable.

Steep canyon walls crowded close to both sides of the roadway. The fingernail moon hid behind the cliffs and made brief appearances whenever the road turned. A creek rushed along beside me. Occasionally, an approaching pickup truck sent reverberations through the canyon, the headlights casting eerie beams up the towering walls. After riding hundreds of miles through open desert, I now felt comforted, cradled between the canyon walls.

As the darkness lifted, the colors and views of cliffs and canyons tempered the extreme work of climbing. Morning light glinted off rock faces of browns and golds and pinks. A profusion of wildflowers graced the roadway; I picked bluebells, lupines, and larkspurs and stuck them on my handlebars, enjoying the cheerful colors fluttering before me.

At a small parking area on Highway 143, I paused to take in the panorama. A deep crevasse opened before me, an amphitheatre of color. Extreme erosion by wind and water had exposed layers of shale, limestone, and sandstone. Spires and cliffs glistened in reds and yellows.

I reached the highest point of my route that day and then savored the next ten miles, a sweet ride downhill through the Dixie National Forest. Leaning over my aero bars, I floated past green mountain meadows interspersed with gnarled bristlecone pine and the white bark of aspen. In the distance, Panguitch Lake sparkled in the late morning sun.

At the Bears' Den Café across from Panguitch Lake, a delicious bowl of southwestern beef vegetable soup revived my tired body. The morning's steep climbs were behind me. I reminded myself of something I had discovered on my hike of the Appalachian Trail—most of my worries never materialized. The unknown often scares and worries us, but most of our fears never come to fruition. A vivid picture filed away in my brain is of the plaque that hung behind my uncle's chair. He was dying of cancer at a young age, but that sign asked, WHY WORRY, WHEN YOU CAN PRAY? When I saw difficulties looming ahead, I determined to pray, instead of worry.

The remaining fifteen miles into Panguitch, Utah, rolled by quickly. It had taken six hours to do those first twenty-six miles and less than three hours to ride the last thirty-two miles. I liked that regimen, riding hard in the morning and coasting through the afternoon; but my days seldom played out so perfectly.

Panguitch is a little town in the heart of Mormon country. I was again welcomed by the sprinkler brigade scattering the precious resource over lush green lawns. Any vacant lots deprived of water were dried and parched.

It was early afternoon and I was looking forward to a soak and a long rest. Much to my frustration, an intransigent housekeeper did not realize the urgency of my afternoon plans. I had already checked in when the front desk clerk told me the room had not yet been made up. The housekeeper was adamant; check in was not until two o'clock, and she refused to clean the room for an early occupant.

Two can play that game, I surmised, and I stretched out on the lobby couch, my tired body redolent with all the aromas produced by a strenuous day. The front desk clerk was immediately on the phone, trying to persuade the housekeeper it would be in her best interest to quickly clean my room. He won the war of words and, in short order, I had my soak.

My plan was for an early start the following day, but all of my plans were about to be washed away.

On the road again at four in the morning, I took Route 89 to Highway 12, one of the most scenic routes in America. That road would take me through Bryce Canyon National Park all the way to the town of Escalante, just outside Escalante Grand Staircase National Monument.

I had the road to myself. Just a sliver of moon shone in the sky, and the headlight attached to my handlebars threw a small circle of light on the roadway ahead. As I neared the turnoff for Route 12, I detected another light on the horizon. It reminded me of the northern lights that had fascinated me that first night in

Utah. These, however, were southern lights. And the light show was lightning flashing in the dark sky.

I had been very fortunate during my first month on the road. No thunderstorms had overtaken me. Other than those ocean mists along the coast, I had not been drenched by precipitation. I hoped this storm was moving in the opposite direction.

I was traveling through Red Canyon, where the Red Canyon bike path runs parallel to the highway. Many bicycle accidents on this stretch of highway had led to the construction of the bike path. I alternated between road driving and trail riding for several miles. When the trail veered away from the road, I'd lift my bike over the rocks and sagebrush and get back on the highway.

These dark, early morning rides were filled with loneliness, and the first rays of sunlight always lifted my spirit. As the first light of dawn sparkled on the red canyon walls, my mind drifted back to another time when I had traveled this road with my wife and family. Had I known then how drastically our lives would change, I would have savored every moment we had together. Instead, I had too often been so focused on goals that the journey sometimes became a distraction. Life is all about seizing today. We need to plan for the future, but not at the expense of missing all the joys and blessings in our lives today.

If it was a lonely and nostalgic morning, it was also a morning filled with awe. Towering cliffs of gold and brown inspired me. It was as if I was traveling through a grand cathedral. This cathedral, however, was not built by human hands. This was a celestial temple.

Morning light also showed that an ominous ceiling covered this outdoor temple. Dark, angry clouds came slinking over the edge of the precipices. That early morning lightning had been a harbinger of the storm that now intersected my path and threatened to dampen my mood.

I pedaled harder, faster, attempting to outrun the dark clouds chasing me. A sign promised a town three miles distant. The race was on. Fortunately, the three miles to the little town of Tropic were all downhill or level, and I dodged under a hotel canopy just as the deluge started. Next door was a restaurant, and I decided to sip something hot while waiting out the storm. I left my bike propped against the front of the hotel, unsecured and unattended.

Enjoying my coffee, I called my friend Ina back in Ohio, simply needing someone to listen to my lament about the weather. Instead of compassion for my plight, Ina was astounded that I had left my bike unattended.

"That's like leaving your child unattended. All your belongings are on that bike. Are you out of your mind?"

Perhaps. But there was a method to my madness. I carried neither a lock nor a cable with which to fasten a building to my ride. I chose to trust people. Most folks are still honest, I believed. In addition, I guessed that anyone intent on thievery would look at my bicycle standing there, unlocked, and conclude that the owner was nearby. As Ina said, no one in his right mind would leave a bicycle unattended. Earlier in my trip, I actually had hoped that someone would steal my ride. Then I could go home.

The storm gradually moved away and I was grateful that I had dodged a drenching. Eight miles farther lay a speck on the map called Henrieville. Here the road curved to the left and the surface became quite rough. The little yellow sunflowers danced on the roadside but carried a message of difficulty ahead, bowing deeply in my direction and warning of a headwind.

For the next several hours I fought not only the wind, but also the grade. I had one more climb of 7,600 feet. After that, the next twenty miles would be downhill into Escalante.

Off to my left was an area with rock formations of a bluish hue, a wilderness area called The Blues. I was also developing a bad case of the blues, both emotionally and overhead. The dark clouds realized I had escaped their wrath back in Tropic, and now they had chased me down once again. There would be no chance of dodging a drenching this time.

I quickly donned my rain gear and stuffed my camera and phone into my panniers. I was about to find out if they were waterproof, as advertised. The rain came in torrents. Lightning flashed around me and thunder reverberated throughout The Blues. Without any kind of shelter, I lowered my head and slowly pushed my bike, walking uphill. I still had a mile to the summit. Streams of water ran along the roadside, soaking my shoes. Passing vehicles added a spray of rainwater to my misery.

At last I shoved my bike to the summit. With a prayer for safety, I jumped on the bike and floated downhill, water spraying all about me. The storm stopped, but my problems persisted. The bike wheels showered me with water and dirt. My face was covered with fine grit. The rain suit blocked my mirror, making it impossible to see anything behind me. My rain gear was black, and the road had no shoulder. I asked God to protect me from any vehicles approaching from the rear.

There was one bit of good news, though. The little flowers had been given much to drink and now bobbed and waved in the opposite direction. The miles were all downhill and I had a tailwind. Gradually, the road surface began to dry and the fantail of moisture and grime decreased. I coasted into Escalante with spirits at low tide.

All I wanted was to check into my room and dry out. I had booked a room in this town. It was a Saturday, and because Escalante was at the edge of these national parks, it had seemed prudent to make a reservation. The lady who made my reservation had informed me that my bicycle would have to stay outside. No bikes in the rooms. I thought that was like saying my wife could stay with me, but the children would have to sleep on the sidewalk.

I rode into town under dark clouds. My shoes and socks were soaked and my spirits sagging. My first impression of Escalante was not favorable, and it would soon sink even lower. I arrived at the motel to find a sign stating that I would not be able to check in for another two hours. My disgruntled state of mind produced a few uncomplimentary remarks about the place; in an agitated conversation with myself, I remember using the word "fleabag" and making a comment on the lack of cleanliness.

I had passed another motel coming into town, and now I decided to see if they could accommodate me. The lady in charge was kind and helpful. She even loaned me a hair dryer to dry my shoes. In the two hours I would have spent waiting at the other motel, fuming and in a deteriorating mood, I instead dried out my shoes, took a soak, and fell asleep in the tub. I did call the first place to inform the proprietor that she would be deprived of my presence that evening.

Later that evening, after a hearty meal, I took a stroll through the town. The sun was now shining and I viewed Escalante in an entirely different light. Quaint old buildings and art shops populated the town and wild flowers bordered the streets. I even spotted several ornate front porches that looked inviting. It is amazing how our viewpoints can change when a situation becomes better illuminated.

That Saturday had been a hard day of riding, and Sunday promised more of the same. The Hogback was ahead of me, a three-mile section running across a narrow spine of rock with drop-offs on either side and no shoulders. I'd heard stories of horror about this section; bicyclists had even been killed in accidents there. My hope was that since it was Sunday there would be less traffic as I crossed the treacherous stretch.

The morning's passage through Escalante Grand Staircase was an incredible ride. At Boynton Lookout, I stopped to take in the inspiring vista before me. For miles the road wended its way through a great outdoor cathedral. I rode in awe and reverence, drifting around curves, admiring fascinating and colorful rock formations, gliding through deep canyons. The inspiration waned somewhat when, at the lowest reaches of the canyon, I realized I would have to work my way uphill again.

The Hogback, like everything else in life, was not as difficult as advertised and my worries never materialized. I met another biker and asked him how close I was to the Hogback. "You're on it," he told me. I had already done two of the three notorious miles.

Then came an eight-hour uphill climb to an elevation of 9,600 feet. When I finally arrived at the Homestead Overlook, the views were stunning. The view of the heavens also stunned me. Several storm fronts were joining forces, and heavy black clouds were heading my way. I quickly pushed off and was blessed with miles of downhill.

Five miles out of the town of Grover I saw the sheet of water heading toward me. I ripped my rain gear from the panniers and was once again the man in black.

This storm was ferocious. I was on level ground, so I could continue pedaling through the mayhem. Water flooded the roadway and pebbles tumbled down the steep banks along the highway.

A honk and a wave from a passing motorist told me I wasn't the only crazy person on the road. The friendly greeting came from the driver of a Mustang convertible. The car's top was down and he, too, was being pummeled by the downpour. This was either a case of mechanical difficulties or maniacal difficulties.

At the intersection of Routes 12 and 24, the little settlement of Torrey bills itself as the Gateway to Capitol Reef National Park. I found shelter there under the awning of a building. While lamenting my misfortune, I noticed a Days Inn a short distance down the road and knew immediately that my day was done.

I took my bedraggled self to the front desk and was pleased to find a friendly proprietor offering a great deal. A motorcycle rider also arrived and announced that this storm had been the worst he had ridden through in his entire life.

I repeated the routine from the day before, going through another wash, rinse, and dry cycle. Although I was twenty miles short of where I had planned to be, I was comfortable and dry. Surely the worst was behind me and tomorrow would be better.

I was wrong, of course.

Because the storms had forced me to end the previous day earlier than planned, I had not reached my goal of Hanksville. Now I had no idea where I might end up at the end of this day. I was still in areas of extreme desolation and lodging was limited.

It always works out, I assured myself.

The morning started off in splendid fashion. A few short miles, and I entered Capitol Reef National Park. It was another exhilarating ride through canyons and giant rock formations. The park is so named because the spires and giant white domes carved out of Navajo sandstone bear a resemblance to the United States capitol building.

Nestled deep between canyon walls is Fruita. The area's early Mormon settlers planted fruit trees here, on 300 acres along the Fremont River. Many varieties of apple, cherry, peach, and apricot trees grow in twenty-two orchards. Today the National Park Service owns these orchards and tends 2,600 trees. Passersby are welcome to have a free snack, but there is a charge to take home a basketful.

Although I had been drenched by rain on only the last two days, the locals told me there had been ten days of rain. The Fremont had overflowed its banks and when I saw a giant beaver ambling along, I surmised that he had been rendered homeless by the flooding. Native Americans called the beaver the "sacred center" of the land because the beaver dams create native habitat for other wildlife. The misplaced rodent I met was now traveling directly on the yellow line in the sacred center of the road. I recalled hikers on the Appalachian Trail who would sometimes travel by car to avoid difficult sections of the trail. They were given the dubious title of "yellow blazers." This beaver slowly slogging down the center of the highway was truly yellow blazing. I feared for its life and gradually shepherded it off to the side of the road.

The storms had misplaced me, too. I had wanted to be in Hanksville the previous night, within reach of Blanding on this new day. But the rain had completely altered my schedule. Blanding was 180 miles from Torrey, an impossible goal for that evening. Instead, I set my sights on the Hite Marina at Lake Powell. That would still be a 100-mile ride; but the skies were cloudless and blue, and the terrain was mostly downhill or flat. I could do it.

From the information I had, lodging at the Hite Marina did not look promising. *But something always works out,* I thought again.

In a valley ringed by flat-topped mesas, I came upon a small, ramshackle building, a market advertising pastries, organic coffee, and freshly baked bread. A coffee break sounded good, and I lifted my bike over the rocks and burrs littering the driveway, walked up the ramp, and announced myself.

With a floppy hat covering long locks, Jack looked like a throwback to the sixties generation. He ground his organic coffee for my beverage, and I asked how he ended up out here in the middle of nowhere.

"I have forty acres here that own me. The Fremont River flows through the back of my property, so I can irrigate my land. I raise goats, and I bake bread and pastries in that stone oven I laid up out back."

"But where were you before ending up here?" I asked, sensing a story.

His answer was something he said he'd heard on a Smothers Brothers show back in the sixties. "If I hadn'ta been there, I wouldn'ta been here."

I suppose we could all say that. If we had not done what we did in the past, we wouldn't be where we are today. I reckoned it was Jack's way of telling me, "It's none of your business what brought me here."

Jack's flock of goats grazed in a field nearby, and he had a three-year-old sheepdog he was training to corral the animals. I sat on the front porch, sipping coffee, and admiring the interaction of owner and dog. The dog, Zeke, was stationed at a gap in the fence, guarding against any attempt at escape by the goats. Unfortunately, the dog was more intent on watching me than the goats, and several of his charges slipped through the gap and went roaming along the roadside. A yell from Jack sent the dog bounding after the escapees. He circled around them and brought them back to safety. I thought it would be easier just to fix the fence, but I kept that thought to myself.

Down the road in Hanksville, I took my time lunching on two hot dogs. The day was extremely hot and I was in no hurry.

At the edge of Hanksville, I left Route 24 and turned south on Route 95, changing direction and now pedaling into a strong headwind. The route led down into a canyon once again, with red walls rising on either side of the highway. The deeper I rode into the canyon, the hotter it became. I pulled off the road and released air from my tires, hoping to avoid another blowout.

The blue expanse of Lake Powell shimmered in the distance. This lake was created when the Glen Canyon Dam was erected on the Colorado River. Above the dam, canyons were flooded and an entire recreational area developed around the resulting 186-mile lake. I had done a river trip through the Grand Canyon with each of my children individually, and each trip had started just below the dam.

I crossed a bridge over the Colorado, just before the river flowed into the lake. A sign pointed in the direction of Hite Marina, my goal for that day. The marina turned out to be just a small visitor center and a little grocery store. Lodging here, rather than being limited, was nonexistent. The clerk suggested that I could sleep on the banks of Lake Powell. I had pedaled 100 miles and wanted to sleep on more than grass.

"Could I possibly continue on to Blanding?" I wondered aloud.

"That's an eighty-mile ride, and most of it's uphill." The shocked look on the clerk's face told me more than her words.

There are good ideas and there are bad ideas. This was not one of my better ideas. But I wanted a bed to sleep in. And I wanted very much to get these long and lonely stretches behind me.

It was already six o'clock in the evening, but I reasoned that if I could ride ten miles per hour, it would be possible to reach Blanding by two in the morning. As I said, good ideas, bad ideas. This was a bad, bad decision.

The sun was setting over the lofty red cliffs. Brilliant orange streaks across the sky announced the ending of the day. It was also the beginning of the longest night of my life.

I soon met a car coming from the direction of Blanding. The young driver, who had a kayak atop the vehicle, stopped and asked if I needed help. I told him I was trying to make Blanding that night.

"You're doing what?" he exclaimed incredulously. "There's nothing between here and Blanding." I assured him I knew that, but I thought I would be okay. He offered me water, and I filled my bottle from a gallon jug he handed me. "You're more man than I am if you pull this off," he said.

At eight o'clock, darkness set in. I flicked on my headlight and nothing happened. Not a ray, not even a glow. Nothing. I inserted the extra set of batteries. Still no illumination. The two days of rain had apparently corroded connections and left me in the darkness. I rubbed, flicked, and manhandled the light till it gave forth a feeble beam. A bump in the road turned it off, and another bump might turn it on. As I rode, it occasionally flared to its full power, then flickered out completely.

Whenever the lamp refused to shine, I found the center or side line on the highway and tried to follow it. But even that pale white line was sometimes difficult to see. Clouds obscured the small sliver of moon and the night grew eerie. Small trees and bushes took on dark and sinister shapes, looming up like misshapen creatures of the night. Throughout the entire night, only two vehicles passed me.

I had stopped for a short break when, in the blackness beside me, I heard heavy movement and snorting in the brush. Yes, I was scared out of my wits. The quietness of the night was ripped by my scream, followed by the sound of pounding hooves. I was in open cattle area and had probably happened upon a herd; but it was so dark that I could not make out any shape or form that might have belonged to the snorts and hooves.

I was so alone. The creature that had been stalking me for many days now pounced, and I had no defense to fight it off. Here in the dark wilderness, abject loneliness hit me with a vengeance and toppled all my resistance. Sadness came with the loneliness and rolled over me with such power that I couldn't even pray for comfort; I could only groan.

I am completely alone out here in the darkness. Worse, no one even knows I am here; none of the people I care about know that I am lonely and desperate and miserable. I am in Utah hell.

I had once before lived through an experience so awful that I thought it must be something like hell. That also happened along the Colorado River, not far from where I now rode.

On my first river trip through the Grand Canyon, our captain had pulled to the riverbank one morning for an excursion into a canyon. Usually these hikes are on well-defined trails, but this was an unmarked walk back to an abandoned miner's cabin. Not everyone on the boat chose to take the hike; and along the way, some who had started decided to turn back. The heat was intense, and we walked along exposed areas where the sun hit us directly. We later learned that the recorded temperature at Phantom Ranch, at the bottom of Grand Canyon, was 120 degrees that day. Only the captain, my daughter, and I reached the mining site. Others had given up the hike and returned to the boat.

On our return, we found one of our group, an older gentleman, lying on the trail. He was one of those who had turned back, but he'd suffered heat stroke and had fallen along the trail. We found him incoherent, with a bleeding face, and out of water.

We were quite a distance from the raft and any assistance. Fearing the man would die if help didn't arrive soon, the captain attempted to radio planes that might be flying overhead, but there was no contact.

I offered to hike back to the rest of the group waiting at the raft. But on my own, far from the river, I lost the faint trail and became disoriented. The day was extremely hot. I walked into a spiny cactus and the blood ran down my leg. Under a rock overhang, I took refuge from the sun and begged God to help me. *Show me how to get back to the boat. And God, if hell is anything like this, help me to live a life to avoid that.*

"Walk to the river," I heard myself say. Hoping to look upriver and spot the raft and thus get my bearings, I clambered over house-sized boulders. But there was only the edge of a cliff, the river far below. No boat in sight. In panic, I clambered back up over the same rocks, and looked frantically for any faint sign of a trail. Finding a marking that looked as though it might be a trail, I followed it.

Back at the boat, the rest of our group was growing concerned at our long absence. One man offered to walk up the slope to see if we were in sight.

The trail I was following was just an animal trail and did not lead back to our boat. But at a distance, I caught a glimpse of the man looking for us, and I knew I would be safe.

I explained the situation to the rest of the group. The captain and my daughter had stayed with the sick man up in the canyon. Two other men and I hiked back with more water and food, and in the cool of the evening everyone returned to safety.

Years later, I met the captain again and we talked of that day. He told me he had been very afraid the man would die in the heat. It had been, he said, the most frightening day of the twenty years he spent as a guide in Grand Canyon.

The day was burned in my memory as the hottest, driest day I'd ever experienced. Add to that the desperation of being lost, not being able to find my way. That must be something of what hell will be like.

And now here I was, just miles east of that same canyon, trying to travel in utter darkness, lonely and cold. Here again I was given a glimpse of what it will be like to be eternally lost in hell. But this horrible misery was one night; morning light would change everything. What would it be like to be forever in such a hell?

I shuddered as I contemplated that. Yet many folks will pass on from this life and be faced with just that destiny. Many who hear the call to salvation but delay their decision will wake up someday to an awful, terrible shock. I cannot comprehend what it means to be forever lost.

"Forever" and "eternal" are words the human mind cannot quantify. We think in terms of *time*. In this life, we measure time in hours, days, months, and years. Our mind wants defined beginnings and endings. We are in this short period of measured time, and our years are just a speck between eternity past and eternity future. Millions of years from now, you will be somewhere in eternity future. You may have made a lot of bad choices in your life, but this can all be remedied by one good choice. The question is, where will you spend eternity?

This is a story of a bicycle trip across America. You might wonder why I need to discuss such subjects now. I can only surmise that God had me right where He wanted me that night and was reminding me of things I needed to contemplate. And since it is such a very important message and perhaps the very reason I had to ride across America, I also offer the message to you.

After fifty miles of climbing, I was again headed downhill. I could not, however, reach any great speed in the darkness. My light still flickered off and on, unpredictable and unreliable. I had found that if I held the light tightly, a feeble glow fell on the roadway. It was almost like squeezing the small beam from the headlight. One hand clutched the light, one hand was on the handlebars.

Nearing the bottom of the hill, I hit a thermal air pocket and the cold was suddenly intense. I donned my rain gear, attempting to stay warm. I was now lonely, sad, depressed, *and* freezing.

Here came another uphill. I was so exhausted that I had no strength to pedal. I pushed. And pushed. And pushed. I pushed my bike for hours. Every now and then, I'd lift the front of the bike, searching with the feeble light, trying to find mile markers. *How much farther?*

I knew I was weaving in the road. My mind started to play tricks on me. I remembered stories about truckers being on the road too long and seeing camels and zebras where there were none. I heard voices; friends were yelling at me. *Paul, get on the bike and pedal!*

At three in the morning, I collapsed. Whimpering like a baby, I lay down in the ditch at the side of the road, rested my head on a rock, and passed out.

A noise jolted me awake. A truck, coming toward me on the highway. I struggled to my feet and climbed on the bike. One by one the miles passed. Within an hour, I spotted several faint lights far off in the distance. I hoped it was Blanding.

In the darkness, I could detect high rock formations beside me; but that was all I knew of my surroundings. Soon, mercifully, a glimmer of light appeared behind one of the cliffs. The lights of Blanding came into clearer focus, too. Although I was still several hours from the end of my ride, the darkness was at last gone. A beautiful sunrise greeted me, beams of light spreading in all directions. I could once again see the flowers blooming along the roadside.

At eight in the morning, I arrived on the outskirts of the town. I had been riding for twenty-five hours. I had witnessed two sunrises and one sunset and traveled 180 miles.

I stumbled through the front door of a motel and collapsed in a chair. The night clerk was still on duty and announced that he was completely full and he could not give me a room before eleven o'clock. Utterly disappointed, I stopped at another motel, only to hear the same thing.

At the far end of Blanding, I finally met a Good Samaritan. After hearing about my ride, she took pity on me and offered to clean the first vacant room. At ten, I collapsed into bed, unable to think about what I had just been through.

In the far recesses of my mind—or was it in my heart and soul?—I was aware something significant had happened on the road to Blanding. Whether the revelations from that lonely, dark night were intended only for me or for someone else, I'll probably never know.

I do know that when you are at your lowest point in life, when you are stumbling about in darkness seeking direction, there is help. Seek the light, follow the light; it will lead out of darkness to everlasting day.

Later, I checked my map. I had no concept of the country I had ridden through during that long night, and I was curious what landmarks I had passed in the darkness. I outlined the stretch I'd done through the wilderness, in black loneliness where no one could help me and where I felt as if I were surely in hell, a stretch that put all of time and eternity into perspective for me.

On those dark miles of my journey, I had crossed a place called Salvation Knoll.

CHAPTER 12

Colorful Colorado

I awoke in two states, the state of Utah and a state of Confusion. It was late afternoon, and I had no idea where I was. Several moments passed before the fog in my head lifted. Had I really biked 180 miles through heat and cold, mountains and desert? I sat on the edge of the bed, reflecting on the how and why of my marathon ride.

I had made a poor choice when I decided to push for Blanding. But the motivation behind that decision was quite simple. I was tired of these empty and desolate stretches. I wanted to pedal as hard and fast as I could, and leave the loneliness far behind. Although I enjoy my own company, there comes a time when conversations with self are not sufficient and other human discourse is needed.

My thoughts had kept me company and helped me through the night. On extended alone times, whether hiking through the wilderness or biking in the desert, I played mind games. I'd pick questions or issues and carry on internal debates. I can debate politics for hours. Have you ever noticed that the further left a person is on the political spectrum, the less likely he is to need or believe in God? Move to the right on the political scale, and you will find more people of faith. Move to the extreme right to find the folks who believe they are God.

I contemplated social phenomena, too. On the road to Blanding, I had weighed the merits of boxing. What is the logic of two men standing in a ring, each pulverizing the other's head? The first person to slump to the canvas in a coma is the loser. Why do folks pay to see this? Boxing seems to be today's equivalent of the ancients throwing men into a lion's den for sport. Those in the lion's den ended up in the lion; the loser in the boxing ring may still be able to walk, but might be almost brain dead.

And consider those sword fights in movies. Mind-numbingly boring. Back and forth go the combatants. Swords clink and clank endlessly. If I were a knight heading for a sword fight, I'd go to the sword shop and order a weapon at least a foot longer than my opponent's and then dispatch him immediately without any clink or clank. Perhaps not a fair fight, but the mind is mightier than the sword.

Great thoughts and debates, both serious and silly, had occupied my mind until the loneliness bugaboo attacked. Then sadness turned my thoughts in a different direction, eastward and homeward. I think our minds seek a place of happiness and safety when confronted by sadness. I followed a wave of memories back to my childhood.

I was again in Mom and Dad's house, playing games with my sisters, sitting around the supper table. Just as memorable were the drives we took in the old '56 Pontiac. Every year we took a much-anticipated trip to the zoo. For several months before the trip, we'd squirrel away candy for that special day. On the morning of our outing, Mom would send me to the garden to harvest a cabbage head which she would slice up as a snack for the trip. On the road to Blanding, my taste buds recalled the sharp tang held in that smooth ball of tightly packed leaves.

Granted, a strange series of debates, thoughts, and recollections accompanied me through the darkness, but my mind had a lot of time and space through which to wander.

Once I was awake and again had my wits about me, a yearning for the taste of cabbage led me to a restaurant with a salad bar. It's amazing how a delicious hot meal can improve one's disposition. The food was excellent; and yes, the salad bar offered coleslaw. Coleslaw is either very good or very bad; there is no middle ground. Good coleslaw is crunchy and bursting with flavor. Bad coleslaw has the texture of a wet, abandoned bird nest. The slaw that night brought a smile to my mouth. The cabbage was crisp and sharp, full of flavors that spoke of a summer growing in the sun.

In my years in food service, we often spoke of comfort food. Give the customer food that reminds him of his childhood, and you will have a repeat customer. That coleslaw was comfort food for me that night. But I would not be a repeat customer; Colorado beckoned in the morning.

I went back to my motel room and slept the night away.

WELCOME TO COLORFUL COLORADO, said the sign. I was traveling on a high plateau, surrounded by color. Fields of yellow sunflowers stretched in all directions, and large grain silos rose from the verdant landscape. Where the soil was exposed, it showed dark red.

My enjoyment of Colorado's hues was darkened somewhat by the storm clouds overhead. The wind had picked up, attacking me broadside and making it impossible to ride in a straight line. I could see the dust storm approaching. A Jeep pulled over and the driver offered me a ride to the next town. I explained about my cross-country ride and that I could not skip any miles. He was kind enough to give me sanctuary and we sat in the Jeep and talked as the dust storm reduced visibility to almost zero.

The man had retired from a thirty-year Army career. His last assignment had been in Iraq, where he worked on a project protecting soldiers from roadside bombs. Now he was beginning his retirement with a trip across the country, visiting national parks. (I had noticed the bike on a rack at the back of the Jeep.) He admired my stubbornness and asserted that he would not skip any miles either, if he was doing such a ride. Our conversation touched on politics, war, peace, and the character of the people we had both met in our travels. The dust swirled around us as I took the opportunity to tell him about Jesus, who is my shelter in times of storm.

I spent the rest of my eighty-two-mile day dodging storm clouds. Just before reaching the town of Dolores, my goal that day, I passed a farmers' market on the main street; and all the fruits and vegetables triggered another summertime craving. After checking into my room at the Dolores Motor Inn, I immediately headed back to the market with one thing in mind. The watermelon was far too much for one person, so I offered half to the front desk clerk. Back in my room, my half of the watermelon filled the sink and my feasting began.

Outside, the rain clouds that had chased me all day converged over Dolores and water poured down all evening and all night. The morning brought a promise of sunshine, even though dark clouds still scurried across the sky.

After the long, dark night in Utah, fields of flowers, clover, and vegetables had gladdened my spirit on my first day in Colorado. This second day was filled with mountain passes and spectacular scenery. Craggy peaks soared into a blue sky as I first followed the Dolores River for several miles then began the climb toward the mountain town of Rico.

A shiny silver disk on the road shoulder caught my attention. I had seen many of these silver CDs in my highway department store, and I always wondered how these ended up on the roadway. Perhaps someone just hated the music so much they tossed it out the window. I could no longer resist. The thin silver circles always reminded me of Frisbees, and now with a quick flick of the wrist, I sent that disk of music sailing. It glided out over the mountainside and made a gentle landing on the banks of the Dolores River. There's more than one way to be entertained by music.

At a small café in Rico, I refueled with a delicious pasta meal and continued my ascent to Lizard Head Pass. At 10,222 feet, a volcanic rock formation juts 400 feet above the mountain, its shape supposedly resembling a lizard's head. If your vision is blurred or your imagination vivid, you might see a lizard. In my view, the formation could just as easily be a horse, an elephant, or an automobile.

Misshapen though it might be, I fell in love with the lizard since it stood at the top of my climb and reaching it meant the next twenty miles would all be downhill into Telluride. With both hands squeezing the brakes to avoid following the path of my CD Frisbee, I descended. It was a euphoric ride, my senses on full alert as I took in the views. Mountain lakes, forested slopes, and expanses of wildflowers all clamored for my attention.

The first seventeen miles were pure biking joy. The final three miles were not so joyful. The roadway into Telluride was crowded, so I pedaled on a bike path following a spur road into the upscale resort town. The bike path was filled with ruts and was most uncomfortable. By the time I reached the center of town, I was quite grumpy; and Telluride did nothing to dispel that mood or win my affection.

This town caters to the rich and elite. I was neither. Many Hollywood stars own properties here, and groupies mill about, hoping to catch glimpses of their heroes. I am not enamored with vacuous and arrogant Hollywood stars and have no sympathy for their hangers-on. I was a party of one in a town filled with snobs.

I stopped at one motel to inquire about a room. They had a special for $250.

"Is there nothing more reasonable?" I queried. The clerk suggested a motel a little farther down the street.

Since the street was crowded and I wasn't traveling far, I rode on the sidewalk. A young man approached, laden with purchases he had made at the expensive tourist shops. With his sweater wrapped around his neck and a jaunty step, he exuded arrogance and self-importance. We did an awkward bob-and-weave on the sidewalk.

He moved left; I moved left. He dodged right at the same moment I did. Apologizing profusely for obstructing his path to the nearest store, I finally darted around him. He turned and screamed at me.

"The road would be a good idea!"

I was extremely tired and grumpy at that moment, and I completely failed this pop quiz in Conflict Resolution 101. I looked back over my shoulder and yelled, *"Then get out on the road!"*

This upset the privileged one greatly. With packages flailing about, he shook his fists and threatened to inflict bodily injury on me. Fortunately there was enough distance between us that I didn't think he could catch me. He would also need to unhinge himself from all the worldly possessions weighing him down, should he decide to pursue me.

Before pushing my bike through the front doors of the New Sheridan Motel on West Colorado Avenue, I paused to take in the spectacular view. Telluride is nestled in a beautiful mountain valley. In the distance, a waterfall cascades snow melt down an immense mountain cliff. I paid dearly for my room, but that incredible view made it less painful.

I fled the town as the first rays of dawn came over the mountains. Since the masses were all still abed, I used the main road for my escape. Although I doubted that Package Boy had ever seen that time of the morning, I wanted to be out of town before he was on the streets looking for me. Only one rude person suggested that I get off the road and use the bike path. I just couldn't please those folks in Telluride. One person insists I get out on the road, and then another yells for me to get off.

I headed for Montrose, Colorado, seventy miles away. In Montrose I would again pick up Route 50, which I would take across the remainder of Colorado and most of the way through Kansas. I was already dreading another climb that was still days ahead of me, Monarch Pass and the Continental Divide.

Monarch Pass was the steepest and tallest climb of my entire trip. I did what I could to prepare for it. Just past Montrose, I stopped at the post office in a small settlement called Cimarron. My third purge of unnecessary items resulted in more weight sent home. I even exchanged ten pennies for one dime.

On the morning of the climb, I took on extra fuel. I had one breakfast in Gunnison, then another in the foothills of Monarch Pass, just before entering Gunnison National Forest.

Then the slow, slow climb began. Every time I passed a mile marker, I shouted with joy. Ride several hundred feet, push several hundred feet. Ride, push, ride, push; that was my pattern for hours. One result of this slow progression was increased net worth. My climb up Monarch Pass netted me eighty-six cents.

Enormous gouges scarred the mountainside, marking sites where rocks had been wrenched out to create space for the highway. The higher I rode, the more grand the view. Mountain peaks rose against a clear blue sky. I caught glimpses of the summit as I rode and pushed, rode and pushed. At last the steep incline leveled off, and a sign announced, MONARCH PASS, ELEVATION 11,312 FEET.

I was also on top of the Continental Divide. The San Isabel National Forest lay on one side of the mountain and the Gunnison National Forest on the other. Somewhere along my route was the precise demarcation between two watersheds. A drop of water landing here yells, "Sorry, gotta split," and then it divides and each half heads off toward its specific ocean. I was happy that I myself was heading toward the Atlantic Ocean.

I was also comforted by the knowledge that this was the highest climb of my entire trip, and now it was done. Those big climbs that I had dreaded so much were behind me. Although they were certainly difficult, my worries about them had proven unwarranted. Those climbs had been conquered by just moving forward, a strategy I have found is the secret of accomplishing many dreaded and difficult tasks.

My forward motion was about to accelerate. The ride into Salida was twenty-five miles of downhill, just as steep and thrilling as the uphill had been steep and arduous. First came ten miles of heart-pounding excitement. Safety hung in the balance as the views distracted my attention from the roadway. No one went by me; I was one with the traffic. I briefly considered passing the car in front of me for the sole purpose of catching a shocked look on the driver's face, but better sense prevailed. Around bends and curves my bike and I barreled. It was thrilling, my mind and body electrified by acute sensations. I will admit, though, it was not just the aspen trees that were quaking on the mountainside that afternoon.

The next fifteen miles into Salida were a gradual downhill, made even easier by a tailwind that pushed me along. I leaned out over my aero bars and soaked in the scenery. I was a human feather floating along, held aloft by a mountain breeze. I was also held aloft by my Dr. Scholl's, which were still working marvelously.

I left Salida the following morning, propelled by great anticipation. The scenery was stunning, with the Arkansas River flowing peacefully on my left and mountain ranges in all directions. By noon I had reached Cañon City, and signs everywhere extolled the wonders of Royal Gorge and the Royal Gorge Bridge, America's highest suspension bridge. On any other trip, I would have taken that side road. But now I wanted to reach Pueblo, Colorado, as soon as possible. In Pueblo, I would meet a friend.

In my previous life, I worked for a company that owned a number of restaurants, inns, and gift shops. Three of the Ohio restaurants were large in size and volume. My friend Mike managed one restaurant in Plain City; another friend, Ivan, directed the one in Walnut Creek; and I was responsible for the third, in Sugarcreek. We were the big three. Whether at restaurant shows, business meetings, or in our private lives, we were friends and comrades. Since our businesses were all similar, we shared thoughts and ideas, frustrations and successes.

Mike was the first one to break from the triumvirate. He had contracted Colorado fever, and the prescription for that malady was a relocation. Seeking fame and fortune, he moved his family to the Boulder area, where fortune was achieved and fame was still being sought. (Perhaps he thought meeting with me on my bike ride could help him in his quest.)

In Pueblo, I checked into a Super 8 just ahead of the storm that had been building for the previous hour. A call from the front desk informed me a Mike wished to see me. How wonderful it was to reminisce with a friend over a juicy steak dinner. We laughed as we recalled stories of our days in food service. Mike even picked up the tab for my steak dinner, confirming that he had indeed been blessed with fortune.

Back in my room, I received another surprise. My friend Ivan was calling. Ivan had been the second member of the troika to leave for greener pastures. His pilgrimage took him to Sarasota, Florida. He had already assembled his fortune, so he was seeking sunshine and new challenges.

I was the last of the big three to throw in the towel. On the very day I left my office at the restaurant and closed the door behind me for the last time, I left to hike the Appalachian Trail, seeking solace after losing my wife to cancer. I sought neither fame nor fortune; I had found my fortune in the friendship of these two men.

Now, just back from a reunion dinner with Mike, I was taking a call from Ivan. He and his wife, Fran, were planning a trip to Kansas. Their son was on the staff of a church in Hutchinson, and he and his wife had just given Ivan and Fran a new granddaughter.

"When will you be riding through Hutchinson?" Ivan wanted to know. The baby had arrived earlier than expected, and now my friends would be in Kansas just as I was riding through that state. What a gift to be biking 5,000 miles and have the chance to meet with both men who had been so helpful in my own career.

Leaving Pueblo was like playing Dodge-Em. I had rejoined Route 50 back in Montrose, but it was no longer the loneliest road in America. I wove delicately through heavy city traffic and around on and off ramps. Finally, after thirty exits, I reached open country again.

By now I considered myself an expert on road conditions, and what I saw ahead was not pleasant. The surface was a brown and red mixture from which little stones rose, creating a bumpy and uneven surface. I suppose the roughness offers some traction in winter weather, but it appeared that I was riding across the top of a large pecan pie.

A few more miles, and road construction brought traffic to a halt. The crew was laying new asphalt, using an aggregate perfect for a smooth bicycle ride. I coasted up to the man who was directing traffic, fearful that he might not let a two-wheeled vehicle through the construction site. To my surprise, he only warned me to be careful and then proceeded to radio ahead and stop traffic in all directions so this one lone bike rider could sail along the perfectly paved surface.

Once beyond all the construction, I had a racetrack. Beautiful, black, freshly laid asphalt with no loose stones or bumps was bicycling bliss. Long stretches with no traffic added to my enjoyment. The incredibly smooth ride was enhanced further by the enjoyable landscape. Here again were those fields of vegetables, extending for miles. Farmers were in the hay fields; the large bales sitting side by side were not wrapped in the white plastic I'm accustomed to seeing, and these looked like loaves of home-baked bread fresh out of the oven.

Aha. What have we here? Off to the right was a large field, filled with an abundance of just what I had been craving lately—cabbages. The field was absolutely bursting with cabbage heads. Would it be wrong to jump the fence and take a bite? I would not pick the cabbage, just gnaw one well-placed mouthful from the side. If I were a rabbit, I would scurry under the fence and munch away. Were I a cabbage worm, I would be in cabbage heaven. I'd scamper up that plant with all sixteen legs in high speed. Were I a beetle, I'd alight on that ball of tightly packed leaves and bite pinprick holes everywhere. If I were a snail, I could slide my slimy self up underneath that plant, hide in its shade, and slowly chew myself full. But I was not a bunny, worm, beetle, or snail; I was a human. I could not steal, not even one bite.

I was recalled from my flight into the insect world by the sound of a truck bumping and rattling along the edge of the field. A pickup jolted from the field and onto the highway several hundred feet ahead of me. Behind it lurched a wagon heaped full of freshly picked cabbages. Just ahead of me, a tantalizing green mound of exactly what I had been craving.

As the truck picked up speed, a minor miracle unfolded. The wind pulled off outer layers of the cabbages and those leaves spiraled away from the wagon and floated to the ground. The faster the truck moved, the deeper the wind dug, peeling off even more layers and littering the highway with the broad leaves.

Thank you, Lord, for this bounty you have provided. I munched on cabbage for many miles, each mile bringing increasingly tender leaves and the sharp taste evoking precious memories of a wonderful home. It was manna from heaven.

I coasted into Lamar, Colorado, at five in the evening, 123 miles closer to Key West. The mountains were behind me, and ahead would be long stretches of flatlands. The morrow would put me in Kansas, one state closer to home.

Cape Trail Beginning

Pacific Coast Driftwood

Olympic Peninsula
Clear cutting

Oyster Boat Crew

Astoria-Megler Bridge

Oregon Coastline

Tillamook Cheese Factory

Grass Seed Harvest in
Willamette Valley

Rocky Oregon Coast

My First Giant Redwood

Avenue of the Giants

Redwood One-log House

Sonoma Wine Country

Golden Gate Bridge

Riding Through San
Francisco Marathon

Folsom Prison's
Gray Walls

Caples Lake

Descending Carson Pass

Sand Dunes between
Fallon and Middlegate

Old Middlegate Station

The Shoe Tree

Evening in the Desert

Morning in the Desert

Roadside Sunflower

Cedar Breaks National Monument

Storm Clouds Over
Bryce Canyon

Irrigated Pasture in Utah

Mesa Farm Market

Approaching Lake Powell

Colorful Colorado

Monarch Pass

Hay Bales

Onion Field

Kansas Stockyard

THE NAMES OF ABOUT HALF OF THE PEOPLE BURIED ON BOOT HILL WERE RECORDED BY NEWSPAPERS AROUND THE STATE. THEY WERE:

ALICE CHAMBERS
MAY 5, 1878
BELIEVED TO BE THE ONLY WOMAN BURIED ON BOOT HILL. HERS WAS THE LAST BURIAL HERE

JACK REYNOLDS
SEPTEMBER 1872
THE FIRST RECORDED KILLING in DODGE CITY. HE WAS SHOT SIX TIMES BY A RAILROAD TRACK LAYER

CHARLES 'Texas' HILL
and
ED WILLIAMS
FEBRUARY 9, 1873
KILLED IN A DANCE HALL BY THE DODGE CITY 'VIGILANCE COMMITTEE'

J.M. ESSINGTON
NOVEMBER 1872
A CARPENTER AND PART OWNER OF THE ESSINGTON HOTEL. SHOT BY THE COOK

EDWARD HURLEY
JANUARY 1873
KILLED IN A SHOOTING SPREE IN A SALOON

UNKNOWN
FOUND HANGING FROM A TREE WEST OF DODGE CITY

McDERMOTT
'PLUGGED' FEB. 1873 BY CASEY, A FRIEND OF EDWARD HURLEY

JOHN WAGNER
DIED APRIL 1878 of WOUNDS DURING SHOOT-OUT With ED MASTERSON

A BUFFALO HUNTER
Named McGILL
SHOT
MARCH 1873

ELLIS Shot By DAVID BURRELL, A BARTENDER IN THE DODGE HOUSE, JULY 1873

CHARLES WHEDON
A BUFFALO HUNTER, SHOT ON SEPTEMBER 10, 1876

Charley MOREHOUSE
A GAMBLER BY TRADE. DIED DECEMBER 1872

FIVE BUFFALO HUNTERS
WHOSE FROZEN BODIES WERE FOUND NORTH of DODGE CITY on FEB. 2, 1873 FOLLOWING a BLIZZARD

BARNEY CULLEN
JANUARY 1873
A RAILROAD EMPLOYEE WHO WAS KILLED DURING A SHOOTING SPREE IN A SALOON

Boot Hill Residents

Kansas Grain Silos

Storage in Salt Mines

Commodore Hotel

Yoder's Market

Kudzu

Cotton Field

Alabama Countryside

Florida's Smooth Shoulder

Happy

Route 1 Through Florida
Keys

Seven Mile Bridge

Seven Mile Bridge at
Sunrise

Journey's End

CHAPTER 13

Heroes and Friends

"**H**ey, buddy, how far am I from the Kansas line?"
I had just checked into a hotel and directed my question
to the owner. Local folks were usually my best source of information about landmarks, roads, and places to eat and stay. This fellow
was clearly underworked and overfed. While his wife seemed to
be doing all the heavy lifting, he was strutting about, chomping
on an unlit cigar.

"Cross the railroad track at the end of town. Several more
blocks, and you'll be in Kansas." Good. I would soon have another
state behind me.

Like the bread crumbs dropped by Hansel and Gretel, a trail
of onions blazed my route down the highway. Every now and then
a ripe red tomato added a bright splash of color or an occasional
pepper appeared in the vegetable mix. My highway-hardware store
had been transformed into a produce market. Why was I craving
pizza this early in the morning?

My peripheral vision caught the sight of a thousand ground-
hogs observing some morning ritual, sitting on their haunches in
precise rows. Once I focused my vision on the field, I realized this
was not an international gathering of woodchucks but hundreds
of burlap bags filled with onions. The only similarity between the

onions and the whistle pigs was that they both dwelled under-ground. A huge mechanical monster dug up the onions, bagged them, and placed the bundles in long neat rows. Later, in the little settlement of Granada, Colorado, I watched in amazement as open trailers piled high with bulk onions were tipped to the side, the onions cascaded out onto a conveyor belt, and workers sorted and boxed the produce according to size.

The portly, cigar-chewing fellow at the motel had assured me Kansas was only a few blocks away. His definition of a block differed considerably from mine. The railroad tracks were thirty-four miles behind me before I crossed the border into Kansas. Perhaps one block equals one hour out on the prairie. After two hours of pedaling, I rolled into the flat, hot, and windy Sunflower State.

My goal for the day was Garden City, but I soon realized that was too aggressive. I stopped for information at a small grocery store in Kendall. A lady advised me that Lakin was twenty-five miles closer than Garden City and the only town she knew of that had a motel. I placed a call to the Ken-Ark Motel; the room would cost me $35, and no reservation was necessary.

The same sign that told me I was in Kearny County also advised that Central Time started here. This was a good time to take a short break. I skidded to a stop, right on time. There are twenty-four time zones around the world; I was straddling two of them. My back tire was one hour behind my front tire. I rolled forward into Kearny County and lost an hour. They say you can't go back in time, but I stepped back into Hamilton County and went back to the hour I'd just passed. Step back, step forward. Hamilton, Kearny, credit, debit. I wondered what time it was in Heaven. No time zones or clocks measure eternity. It's always *now*.

I was just killing time. But my thoughts were more somber as I pedaled forward, losing an hour of time, and reflecting on how often we are so busy working for a living that we have no time left to really live. Dale Carnegie once said, "One of the most tragic things I know about human nature is that all of us tend to put off living. We are all dreaming of some magical rose garden over the horizon instead of enjoying the roses that are growing outside our windows today."

I want to come as close as possible to living in the now. I didn't have roses gracing my pathway that day, but I did have thousands of little yellow sunflowers brightening my journey. Every day of this trip had brought new moments of life and meaning. Scenes of great beauty had inspired me. Fields brimming with fruits and vegetables brought me joy. Even in those dark desert nights, the heavens had held messages for me.

The best lessons, though, were brought to me through the people I met. The morning I rode into Kansas, a man inspired me without saying a word. The encounter left me moved and humbled.

I was miles from any town and complaining to myself about the wind and the heat, when I saw him coming toward me on the opposite shoulder of the highway. He was in a motorized wheelchair; a breathing tube entered his throat and an oxygen tank lay across his legs. A brace held his head and neck immobile, and his arms were strapped tightly to the chair. His body appeared locked in paralysis except for the fingers of his left hand, which lay on a toggle switch that operated the chair.

He could not turn his head left or right; yet as we passed, his eyes met and held mine for several seconds and I knew I had met a hero. How many of us in that situation would be sitting at home, wallowing in self-pity? I had been grumbling about the weather; this man faced far more obstacles, yet here he was, zipping down Route 50. I had no idea why he was trapped in this chair; but I did know how he had reacted to his lot in life.

There were actually two heroes on the road that day. Behind the wheelchair came a rider on a bicycle, a person who was giving of his precious allotted time to watch over the traveler.

The man in the wheelchair and this wanderer on a bicycle exchanged one glance and each caught a glimpse of the other's soul. In that brief instant of measured time, our spirits met and recognized each other. Many things were passed across the roadway in

141

that one look, things that have no words, things that I cannot yet define or articulate. I don't know yet what all those things were, but I do know that I will know someday. With the passage of time, I expect to understand everything our spirits shared in that one moment.

Whenever I thought nothing more could surprise me, the road would offer up yet one more amazing thing. That day, I happened upon a stretch of highway decorated with little blue butterflies. Thousands of fluttering blue wings waved gently on the road and shoulders; thousands more spiraled through the air above. I suspect the butterflies were taking advantage of all the produce littering the highway. I dodged and swerved through the teeming blue mass; but sadly, some of the fragile creatures met their demise in spite of my cautious driving.

In Lakin, I checked into my $35 room. The motel was old and dilapidated, bordering on uninhabitable. My $35 did give me a bathtub, a bed, and an air conditioner that produced both moderately cool air and disagreeable noises. Next door at Benny's Grill, I had a delicious $6 spaghetti dinner and decided I had received satisfactory value for my dollars spent in Lakin. That spaghetti dinner was worth $35 and the room was worth $6. Things have a way of evening out.

Leaving Benny's, I met a dad with three daughters. The Spirit within often nudges me to speak to someone, although many times I question that prompting. On this evening, the directive was clear: *Talk to that family.* The Spirit must have also opened wide the doors of communication, because the man freely shared that cancer had recently claimed the life of his wife and the children's mother. I assured them that God knows their pain; and although it might seem impossible when in the depths of grief, healing does eventually arrive.

Before returning to my luxury suite, I wandered across the parking lot to a truck stop to buy treats and pastries for the following morning. Two Peterbilt semi trucks sat in the parking lot, engines growling. Their gleaming chrome grilles were adorned with hundreds of blue wings. All those fragile splashes of color that I had so carefully avoided had met their demise in a head-on crash with these huge beasts.

You've probably heard people use the phrase "get out of Dodge" when they are talking about leaving a place, often hurriedly. My goal for the next day was to "get into Dodge." Dodge City, the rough town of the Old West, was my next stop.

While no longer the Wild West, this area is still cattle country. The previous day, I had pedaled past vegetable fields and acres of aromatic alfalfa. Now the hay fields were replaced by large stockyards, and the smells heavy on the air were produced by thousands of cattle corralled in areas where not one blade of grass survived. Hundreds of acres of green had been obliterated by countless hooves. Invariably, each stockyard had a large mound of muck where a lead cow stood on the peak. I imagined it was encouraging the assembled crowd to stay calm, everything would be fine, of course there's no grass, but they're bringing us food and water…

I enjoy a good hamburger or a juicy steak as much as the next fellow, but I was dismayed by the abysmal conditions.

I passed many grain mills. Pausing beside one large complex, I breathed in the smells that brought back warm memories of days I'd tag along with Dad. Familiar sounds of machinery grinding grain were sounds of home. Smells and sounds have an astonishing power to transport us to other places and times.

On the outskirts of Dodge City, a group of cowboys, swinging lariats, came riding over a small hillock. The scene was a monument, the history and spirit of the town caught in still life. Dodge was known as the Wickedest City in the West during its heyday. A major hub of cattle trading, it also attracted railroad workers, buffalo hunters, soldiers, and drifters. Saloons and lawlessness were the norm. Many grudges were settled by gunfights, and a cemetery called Boot Hill was set aside to bury the deceased rascals. Lawmen were hired to police the town; the two most famous, Bat Masterson and Wyatt Earp, became legendary figures who helped populate Boot Hill and slowly restored order in Dodge City.

I pedaled down Wyatt Earp Boulevard, seeking shelter and relief from the heat and wind. My enterprising mind wondered why there were no windmills here; the only mills I'd seen were the feed mills, but the power of the Kansas wind could certainly generate a great deal of energy. I had washed my biking shirt and shorts (being careful to remove my Dr. Scholl's first) and then tossed the clothes over a bush outside the motel. The breezes dried them more quickly than any electric dryer ever could.

Seeking trouble, I strolled down the boulevard. Sure enough, I walked into a gun battle. There was lots of shooting and yelling, and a dead guy sprawled on the grass. The sheriff arrested the shooter, who of course denied any involvement. He tried to convince the sheriff that the dead man had accidentally shot himself— four times.

I wandered past that reenactment, up the hill behind the Boot Hill Museum to the Boot Hill Cemetery. Wooden markers on the graves noted the scoundrels' names and causes of death. Alcohol consumption was a factor in the demise of many. Shootouts seemed to be the only way of settling things in those wild days.

The cemetery did not hold me for long; my thoughts and plans were focused on the living. My friend Ivan was at his son's home in Hutchinson. Tomorrow I would ride toward Hutchinson and get as close to that goal as possible. Then Ivan would drive out to meet me and take me back to son Eric's house for a needed break. I had not had a day off since San Francisco, and I looked forward to good food and good conversation.

I would need an early start to get within range of Hutchinson the next day. At five in the morning, I was the first person getting out of Dodge. My feeble light cast a faint beam on the dark highway. Far off in the distance, red lights flashed on and off, on and off. They reminded me of airport runway lights, except that I detected no air traffic. Twenty miles later, the faint morning light revealed a fantastic sight. Sixty-seven huge wind turbines slowly revolved in the Kansas breeze. Looking like a white forest of towering trees, The Spearville Wind Energy Facility is a wind farm that covers 5,000 acres of wheat fields. The turbines reach a height of 391 feet, and each sits on an acre of land. More turbines are scheduled to be built here; this flat area of Kansas is known as the windiest area in America and could quite possibly become a leading source of wind-generated energy.

Past the turbine forest, I spotted a medieval castle. The sun was just peeping over the citadel's square towers and protecting walls, outlining its turrets against the pale morning sky. As the sun rose higher and I pedaled closer, I realized it was nothing as magical as a castle, but only a group of large concrete grain silos that had been silhouetted by the early morning sun. Perhaps the Kansas heat and wind were affecting my imagination.

It was not my imagination, though, that spotted friendly faces in a pickup truck later that afternoon. I was at mile number 99 for the day when the truck pulled alongside me and offered me a ride. It was my friend Ivan and his son Eric.

"Ivan, you don't really expect me to finish today one mile short of 100, do you?" He understood my logic, and I rode one more mile closer to Hutchinson before loading my bike into the truck and heading into town for time with friends.

I felt blessed that night, sitting at the supper table, eating great food Fran and Karmen had prepared, enjoying the conversation of good friends. It reminded me again that good friends are to be cherished.

The next day, Saturday, Ivan took me and my bike back to the exact spot where he had picked me up the day before. Eric and his friend Jeremy rode with me that day. We made seventy miles, reaching Newton. Then Ivan again transported us back to Eric's home.

On Sunday morning, I attended all three services at the church where Eric served on the pastoral staff. Hopefully, that made up for all the Sunday services I'd missed while on the road. I was greatly relieved to find that the pews were padded, because Dr. Scholl had also taken the day off.

We spent the afternoon underground. Hutchinson gained the nickname of Salt City after salt was discovered under the town in the late 1800s. Mines have been in operation ever since, and we spent the afternoon 650 feet below the city, touring one part of an underground network that extends for sixty-seven miles. At the Kansas Underground Salt Museum, an elevator took us down through the darkness; then a motorized vehicle drove us deep into the caverns. Huge columns of salt were left standing at strategic places to keep the mined area from collapsing.

In areas where mining is finished, the cavern is used as a vault. With a perpetual temperature of 68 degrees and low humidity, this cave is perfect for storing valuables. Stacks of boxes hold medical records and important documents. Hollywood stores memorabilia here. The original prints of the movies *Gone with the Wind* and *The Wizard of Oz* are kept here, along with thousands of other movies. Even foreign countries have storage areas in this underground vault.

The day ended with pizza and watermelon and more good times with friends. The weekend had been like a midflight refueling. Weariness and loneliness, like that Kansas wind, had been conspiring against me, making the pedaling more difficult. The respite with friends had revived me.

Still, it was with a heavy heart that I went back to my solitary ride on Monday. I felt even more keenly how very alone I was on this journey across America.

Ivan drove me back to Newton, where I had ended Saturday's ride. The stretch ahead of me now was through large farming tracts with no stores or settlements until I reached Cassoday, thirty-eight miles away. A gentleman I'd spoken with the previous day had told me that I was heading into an area that even God didn't know existed. It was a lonely ride, but I passed several churches and surmised that God did know about this area, after all.

The very small town of Cassoday proclaims itself the Prairie Chicken Capital of the World. With less than two hundred residents, it may well have more prairie chickens than people. I did find a small grocery store, and I took a short break before pressing on.

I now traveled on the back side of beyond, along miles and miles of corn fields. Scattered farm buildings gave evidence that some human presence was here, but I didn't see much more than fields, a few horses, and the oil pumpers that nodded greetings as I pedaled by. A few gentle hills foretold the end of this state's flat terrain, but the ferocious Kansas wind still opposed my progress.

My stop that night was in the small village of Eureka. My bike had now rolled through three towns with this name, one in California, another in the middle of the Nevada desert, and now this in the eastern part of Kansas. Another $35 was well spent; I had arrived in town just ahead of a thunderstorm.

I was more than ready to leave Kansas, but still had a long day's ride to the Missouri line. Leaving early in the morning, I fought my way toward the border. A nasty wind from the northeast slowed my progress and black clouds in the west chased me. Twenty miles later, still ahead of the rain, I stopped for refreshment and information at a small, rundown café named Lizard Lips.

Here my route turned southward and the wind lessened. The rain, however, finally caught up with me. Fortunately, it was only a light drizzle, and I went through several wash-and-dry cycles throughout the morning as I rode through little prairie towns named Toronto, Coyville, Benedict, Chanute, and Walnut. My goal was Girard, the first town that appeared large enough to have a motel.

At eight o'clock I arrived in Girard as a brilliant red sun slid toward the western horizon. I was dismayed to find that the town of several thousand people had no motel, and so my day was not yet finished.

Fifteen miles southeast was Pittsburg, Kansas. I had no choice but to go on. I had come into Girard on Route 47. In town, Route 7 turned south toward Pittsburg, but before I reached that intersection, my brain stopped working. I rode right by the turnoff for Route 7 and continued east on 47.

Soon daylight was completely gone; the sky was still cloudy and I had only an occasional glimpse of the moon. In the darkness, I suddenly felt the road surface change. A road crew had cut grooves in preparation for repaving. I bumped along, the bicycle shaking and rattling so much that I feared a blowout. Finally I dismounted and pushed, hoping this stretch would soon end.

For the next four miles, I pushed my bike through the darkness. Vehicles blew past me, raising clouds of dust. It had been a day of misery, and my spirits were almost as low as they had been on that long night in Utah.

A truck came out of the darkness and pulled up beside me. The driver rolled down his window.

"I just passed you, going the other direction, and something told me I should stop. Do you need help?" His headlights had picked up the sight of a tired man pushing a bike, and he assumed I had a flat tire.

"I'm just trying to get past this miserable stretch of road," I said.

"I'd be glad to give you a ride."

It was a most tempting offer.

"I can't. I'm on a cross-country bike ride. And I have to ride or push every mile. But tell me—how far am I from Route 126?"

Route 126 was the turnoff from Route 7 that would take me to Pittsburg.

"You're nowhere near 126."

"I thought if I took Route 7 from Girard, then took a left on 126, it would take me to Pittsburg."

"But you aren't on Route 7. You're on Route 47."

In the dark night, I was headed in the wrong direction. If God had not sent that gentleman into my life, I would have turned left at the next road crossing and pedaled off into the unknown darkness, north instead of south, most likely ending up in Nebraska or Iowa.

The driver gave me directions to Pittsburg. The lights of the town finally came into sight, and a yellow glow from golden arches signaled civilization was near. I had biked 124 miles in fifteen hours. Day 46 ended at last.

The elements in Kansas were most unfriendly, but the people of the Sunflower State had been more hospitable than those in any other state I'd traveled through. Some stores keep autograph books for bikers to sign. Clerks offer to fill water bottles with ice. And some folks stop on a dark night to help weary strangers.

CHAPTER 14

Roads Chosen

I was riding down Broadway, searching for Route 126. This would be my road into Missouri, and I knew that here in Pittsburg it ran concurrently with East Fourth Street. Only a few more miles, and I'd cross another state line.

I asked a man on the sidewalk how far I was from Route 126.

"Oh, you still have a long ways to go," he said. "It's way out on the other side of town."

Several miles later, I was on the outskirts of Pittsburg and realized my informant had lied to me. I turned around and backtracked to the downtown area where I stopped a lady and asked where I could find Fourth Street. She pointed to an overhead sign directly ahead of me. I had been just a few blocks away from Fourth Street when I was misdirected. Usually I could count on locals for accurate information, but on occasion I met someone who acted like a jerk.

I had also met one on Route 47 the evening before. The day was almost over and I was hurrying to get into Girard before dark. The road was quite busy and the shoulder very narrow. A semi truck edging close to my lane blasted the horn just as he was upon me, and I almost jumped out of my skin.

On the Oregon coast, early in my journey, a truck driver had pulled the same stunt and had literally scared me off the road and down over a slope. Fortunately, the incline was not too steep and I regained control of the bike. I wonder if the driver had a chuckle when he looked in his mirror and saw me disappear down that bank.

Riding thousands of miles was training me to be an expert at interpreting the intentions of drivers. Those sadistic drivers were few. Sometimes drivers let out long blasts of the horn, expressing their displeasure at being inconvenienced by a bicycle. Many gave a friendly short toot, and I imagined that they wished they could be riding, too.

Once I found my route in Pittsburg, I pedaled only a few miles and entered Missouri. During the last days in eastern Kansas, I had been plagued by a headwind. Now I realized that Kansas was not entirely responsible for those troubles; the stiff breezes were originating here in Missouri.

I was on a small, paved county road that ran through farming country. Large corn and soybean fields bordered my route. Farmers were cutting corn and filling grain bins. Unlike Kansas, where vast concrete silos loomed over the landscape, Missouri farmers had round metal storage bins in a variety of sizes. I stopped several times that morning to admire beautiful farm scenes. At one farm, I watched as silage was unloaded by large augers that emptied into the tops of the shiny bins. The morning sun glinted off the metal walls as the workers hurried about their activities, quite unaware that a solitary biker looked on from a distance.

I was looking ahead with great anticipation to the small town of Golden City, thirty-six miles down the road. The grapevine raved about Cooky's Café, a restaurant on the main thoroughfare through Golden City. You have to try their pies, folks advised.

Cooky's turned out to be a mom and pop operation filled with local farmers and ranchers. A glass case held mouthwatering pies. Apple, peach, and cherry double-crust pies looked delectable. Tins filled to overflowing with cream pies made a choice difficult.

152

The meat loaf dinner was great and the coleslaw perfect. It was time for pie. I had narrowed it down to two contenders. The coconut cream tempted me with its golden, toasted coconut. But there was one pie that I was compelled to taste, a masterpiece called chocolate pecan, combining the tastes of two of my favorite pies. The dessert was as delicious as the name promised. It reminded me of the road surface I had traveled somewhere back in Colorado.

At the center of Golden City, the county road intersected with Route 160. This new route would take me to my evening's destination of Springfield, Missouri. From Springfield, I would take Route 60 across Missouri and through the Ozark Mountains. I knew these mountains would be nothing like the mountains I'd climbed in the West, but the terrain was already rolling and I once again enjoyed the thrill of reaching thirty miles per hour on downhills.

Shortly after six o'clock, I arrived at the western edge of Springfield and stopped at a new Baymont Inn. The front desk clerk was sneaking a smoke break beside the main entrance; she apologized profusely when I coasted up, explaining that the hotel had just opened and things were still quite stressful. I assured her she could take her time and proceeded to tell her about my ninety-five-mile ride in Missouri that day.

"This place looks quite fancy, probably too pricey for me," I observed.

"Come inside," she said. "You were so considerate about my smoke break; I'll give you every deal possible." She offered me the company's lowest corporate rate, and I had a night of upscale lodging.

The money I saved on lodging, though, was quickly spent on food; I called a nearby restaurant and ordered a steak dinner delivered to my room. Missouri was getting quite hilly, after all, and I needed rest and plenty of nourishment.

Springfield is the third largest city in Missouri, and I was just another traveler in the morning rush hour traffic. Finally, after fifteen miles of harrowing maneuvers past on and off ramps and through construction, I arrived on the eastern side of Springfield. The roadsides were again decked with wildflowers bobbing in the breeze. I was now in hilly territory, and in some places the highway had been cut through the hillside and cliffs, leaving rocky walls hugging the road.

In Seymour, Highway 60 changed. Two lanes expanded to four, and I noticed a familiar pattern on the shoulders. Grooves worn by many hooves and telltale trails of buggy wheels told me I was in Amish Country. Serenity soaked through me. I could almost imagine I was home, taking a bike ride in my own Amish community.

One thing was quite unlike home, though. My daydreams were interrupted by a piercing whistle. On the railroad track parallel to the road, a long train rumbled toward me. The lonely train whistle that had so fascinated me as a boy had been much more enchanting at a distance; only yards away, the sound was now a shrill screech that assailed my ears. I paused to absorb the fierce rumblings of the five monstrous iron horses as they roared by. The train stretched out toward the horizon. I counted all 135 loaded coal cars as they passed. Four modes of transportation ran side by side here; bicycles, buggies, cars, and trains had all been tested by time and were all still viable.

The train passed and I resumed my toil against the wind. After seventy-five hard miles I arrived at the intersection of Routes 60 and 95 in Mountain Grove. In the distance, a sign announced Schrock's Motel and Restaurant; I headed toward both a room to sleep in and the potential for good food and good conversation.

I had enjoyed the changing landscape on this second day in Missouri. Scenic vistas of rocks and hills and wooded areas seemed even more beautiful after my stint in the flat farmlands of Kansas. Several times during the day I had pulled off the road to take in the scenes at lumber yards, admiring the rows of sawed hardwoods and breathing in the smells of sawdust and new lumber.

This area seemed more heavily populated with churches. Many had signs out front with humorous phrases containing some nugget of truth. In Cedar Gap, I noticed one sign that said, "GOD EXPECTS SPIRITUAL FRUITS NOT RELIGIOUS NUTS."

Other signs posted in fields carried an angrier tone. Apparently the Missouri Department of Transportation had upset folks in this area. I didn't know what the disagreement was, but dozens of homemade signs denigrated MoDOT. I decided to consult with the local grapevine to satisfy my curiosity.

Schrock's Restaurant was quiet in the early morning. When I walked in, only one other table was occupied. I immediately recognized the importance of this group; the local intelligentsia was meeting. Every small town eating house has such a group. We often accuse the female gender of gossip and rumor mongering, but there are not many ladies who can hold their own against a table full of men. At such a gathering, the truth rides in the back seat and exaggeration drives the vehicle.

After finishing breakfast, I approached the table and apologized for interrupting such an important social gathering.

"I'm riding across the country on a bicycle, and I need information about what's ahead," I explained. "Can you recommend a good place to stop tonight? The map shows a number of small towns, but I don't know where I'll find a motel."

They all agreed that Van Buren would be the logical place to stay. The town was about eighty-five miles east, and stopping there would set me up to reach Sikeston, Missouri, on the following day.

One of the group introduced each of the four. He himself was a banker, one was a carpenter, another a state representative. "And this," he said, motioning toward the oldest member of the group, "is our town half-wit. He keeps himself busy planting trees and bushes around our community."

The gentleman thus introduced seemed accustomed to such a portrayal and never said a word of rebuttal. I had noticed that during breakfast he had spoken very little while the other three conversed loudly. I suspected he was the smartest of the group. Those quiet ones who sit and listen are usually the smartest among us. Those who know that they know are content to be silent in their wisdom. Those who are ignorant often confirm their ignorance by speaking.

I thanked them for the advice and wished them luck in fixing the world. Once I was back on the road, another nasty MoDOT sign appeared in a field and I realized I had missed a golden opportunity to get the truth about the conflict; I could have asked the state representative back at the restaurant.

By midmorning I needed a soft drink break. In the distance, a canopy covering many gas pumps appeared to be the site of a large truck stop. I wheeled in; the sign said OPEN but the place looked abandoned. Coasting past the twenty gas pumps, I saw they all had been shut off. The building itself was in disarray. I wandered inside and was met by an older gentleman.

"Everything is for sale here," he said. "I'm going out of business." I made a sympathetic comment about the economy hurting so many people. "It wasn't the economy that killed my business, it was MoDOT."

That statement got my attention.

"I've seen those signs everywhere attacking MoDOT," I replied. "What did they do to upset the local population?"

"Several years ago, they put this four-lane highway in and made it limited access. That cut my traffic in half; anyone going in the other direction could no longer stop here. Other businesses were also affected. Several farmers no longer had access to some of their fields. I fought MoDOT in court for years and ran up several hundred thousand dollars in legal bills. It turned into a vendetta for MoDOT officials; they just dug in their heels and refused to cooperate." The court finally gave the man the right to construct an access road so that both lanes of traffic could get to his business, but he had to build the road himself. That construction cost him a quarter million dollars, and that cost plus the legal bills he had piled up proved to be too much of a burden.

"My family ran this place for generations. We used to employ twenty-five people. A tornado leveled the business one time, but we rebuilt. I have always been a survivor, but this MoDOT fight wiped me out."

It was another instance of ignorance and stubbornness ruling the day. Too often we elect folks to office who have never held an actual job and have no idea of the inconveniences and burdens they heap on good businesses by foolish political choices made in some stuffy office buildings. Perhaps elected officials need to spend more time at a local eatery playing the half-wit and just listening. In the future, we would be wise to elect folks that are at least half-witted. What an upgrade that would be.

There was a final injury. After all the damages MoDOT had inflicted on the local economy, they were now threatening legal action against folks for the insulting signs.

That afternoon I witnessed another sad picture of America's current economy. I was waiting in line to pay for snacks. A man was speaking with the clerk, and I could hear the desperation in his voice.

"What's happening with my job application?"

"Sorry," came the reply. "We're not hiring right now."

"I have to find a job. I just have to find work." His voice choked and I saw the tears in his eyes as he turned and walked out.

The value of a job is so underestimated by our government officials. A person needs a purpose in life, a reason to get out of bed in the morning. I had seen it time and again on this ride through America. People were desperate for work.

My home community has been more fortunate than many other places during economic downturns. Unemployment is low. God has blessed us with many resources. Yes, there are folks who readily turn your little molehill into a mountain, but there are just as many that will come to your aid should trouble befall you. Many helpless, hopeless folks out there in America have no place to turn in their times of desperation. Friends, we need to thank God daily for all the blessings He has given us.

Van Buren was still fifteen miles away and the afternoon was fading. I needed one more break. While guzzling a can of Mountain Dew, I was approached by a man who entered the store and seemed to recognize me.

"Hey, I just passed you out on the highway. Where are you heading?"

"I hope to end up in Key West, Florida, in a month, but tonight I'll be in Van Buren. Do you know of a good place to eat there?"

He did have a recommendation. All of his life, Dave had been a customer of a restaurant called the Float Stream; and since it was Friday, the eatery would be having a seafood buffet. I pedaled toward Van Buren with a sense of urgency, thinking of that seafood buffet.

I checked into the Hawthorne Hotel in downtown Van Buren. It was a 1950s horseshoe-shaped motel with a swimming pool anchoring the center courtyard. The place was rundown and inexpensive, but it was home for the night.

A short walk down the street brought me to the Float Stream restaurant, on the banks of the Current River and across the street from the Carter County courthouse. Boaters and kayakers use the area for access to the river. The Current is fed by the Big Spring, one of the world's largest free-flowing springs. It spews 286 million gallons of fresh water a day into the river, and the flow has been measured as high as 1.3 billion gallons a day. The Current River then flows into the Black River which in turn flows into the Mississippi. Perhaps instead of trying to squeeze 16 billion extra gallons of water from the desert, Las Vegas should start negotiating with the good folks of Missouri.

The seafood met and exceeded my expectations. Fried fish, shrimp, scallops, and all manner of sea critters filled the buffet. I even tasted fried okra for the first time in my life. The salad bar was fresh and the coleslaw was done right.

As usual, I enjoyed talking to people I met. When my server discovered I was riding to Key West, she explained that her boyfriend's dad had just been buried last week. He was from Van

Buren but had been a scientist working in Key West. Cancer had claimed him at age forty-nine. I told her about my own loss to cancer and the peace and healing I had found while hiking the Appalachian Trail.

The owner of the Float Stream stopped by my table to tell me she had been looking for me. Dave had eaten there earlier in the evening and had told her about meeting me. I complimented her on a well-run restaurant and told her about my own experience in food service. My bike ride could easily have ended in Van Buren. She offered me a job; or, if I'd prefer, she would have even sold me the restaurant. I considered it for a fraction of a second before declining. I was, however, reminded that what I missed the most about food service was the people.

While I was talking with the owner, a man sat down at the next table and she introduced him as the mayor of Van Buren. He was meeting several folks there and invited me to join him while he waited. The best thing that came of our conversation was his recommendation that I stop at the local ice cream shop on my way back to the Hawthorne Hotel. "They have the best ice cream around," he said.

I had seen the signs out on the highway. KIDS, SCREAM TILL DAD STOPS AT JOLLY CONES, the signs advise. The ice cream shop was a small, nondescript building with a large canopy covering a number of picnic tables. I joined a long line and ordered a chocolate sundae with chocolate syrup. While savoring my rich cup of calories, I took in the scene. Close to fifty adults and children sat at the picnic tables, enjoying their food and conversation. Kids ran from table to table, interacting with friends.

This was the America I was hoping to discover—families having fun, laughing, and talking to each other. I was reminded of my walk down the streets of Dalton, Massachusetts, on the Fourth of July during my Appalachian Trail hike. That day I decided to ride across America in search of the soul of our country. Here it was in Van Buren, Missouri. What holds this community together is what holds any home, church, or community together—love and acceptance. The only true source of love comes from God. When we honor God, we will also honor our families and communities. Any nation that rejects God will fall into disarray. Any half-wit could tell you that!

I needed one more product to complete my day. At a small grocery store, I purchased a can of Coke and my day ended as well as a day can end—with chocolate and Coca-Cola.

My last full day in Missouri would be a ninety-eight-mile ride. The temperatures approached the mid-nineties, but the wind had died down and the miles passed by quickly. I pedaled through the towns of Poplar Bluff and Dixon on my way to Sikeston.

I was confused about just where in Sikeston my route would lead. My map showed Route 60 ending at the intersection of two interstates. Interstate 55 headed north toward St. Louis, while Interstate 57 headed east and then north. Eighteen miles east of Sikeston on I-57 was the town of Charleston, Missouri, where I wanted to pick up Route 60 again to cross the Mississippi and the Ohio Rivers into Kentucky.

Coming toward me, on my road shoulder, were two old relics. An old man wobbled toward me on a bicycle that reminded me of my old Roadmaster. I hollered a greeting. It also served as a warning, since he was on my shoulder and coming straight at me. He was obviously startled.

"Who's there?" he asked, and we both stopped.

"I can't see well, and I don't hear so well," he told me. That explained why he apparently had not seen me coming. "I've been ill for some time, and this is my first bike ride in quite a while. What time is it? I lost my glasses and my watch back on the highway somewhere."

Seeing and hearing are two attributes useful for safe bike riding, I thought.

"Do you need help?" I asked. He seemed confused, and I feared for his safety.

"No, I live just a few miles down the road. I've lived in this area all my life and I'm quite capable of finding my way home. Where are you headed, young feller?"

"I'm heading for Key West, Florida, but I'll be in Sikeston tonight." I mentioned that I was planning to eat at a restaurant called Lambert's. "I believe this road I'm on will take me right past it," I said confidently.

"It won't," he said emphatically. I insisted that it would. "Young man, I've lived here over eighty years and I knew the people that built that restaurant. I was here when it was just a small café. I know exactly where it is. You go fifteen more miles, and at the intersection of 60 and 61, you turn left onto 61. Take that to Malone Street and hang a right and that will take you to the restaurant."

He could barely see or hear, he had somehow lost his glasses and watch, and he was on the wrong side of the road. Should I follow his directions? He might have sensed my hesitation.

"Have you ever heard of the magazine *Ford Times*?" he asked. I knew it well. When I was a boy, my father used to bring home that magazine from the feed mill. The periodical was published by the Ford Motor Company and sent to owners of Ford trucks. "Back in the early sixties, there was an article about Sikeston in that magazine," the old man went on. "It was a story about an intersection in Sikeston where three consecutively numbered highways intersect. Routes 60, 61, and 62 all meet at one intersection."

This convinced me the old man did indeed know Sikeston. I thanked the old-timer for the information; and as we parted company, he called out, "Look for my watch, would you, young feller? Keep it, if you find it."

Just as the old man had said, Route 61 appeared and a left and a right did take me past Lambert's Café to an interchange where I booked a room for the night.

A short stroll back up the street took me to Lambert's Café, the home of Throwed Rolls. Servers walk through the restaurant with freshly baked rolls. The cry goes out, "Hot rolls!" If you want a roll, just raise your hand and a roll will come flying in your direction. The roll tossers are deadly accurate. All evening, dinner rolls were called up yonder and flew about me. Other servers walked around carrying pots of potatoes and other vegetables, offering samples to anyone not full of rolls.

I was one full and contented biker when I walked back to my room that Saturday evening. I was looking forward to the morning. Even though I'd been in church services only one time on this trip, Sundays were still special days out here on the road. Perhaps because Sunday traffic was not as heavy as weekday traffic. Perhaps I was more open to inspiring or reverent or thought-provoking experiences simply because it was Sunday.

If nothing else, on the next day I would be entering Kentucky; and that thought delighted me. I would also be meeting several folks the next day. One meeting was on my schedule; the other encounter was something God had scheduled that I as yet knew nothing about.

When I pushed my bicycle into the lobby early on Sunday morning, I paused to chat with the lady at the front desk. She asked where I was headed, and I explained my trip across America; but when I told her the circuitous route I intended to take to Charleston, she offered a suggestion.

"It would be easier and quicker to take the interstate down just one exit to I-57."

"Interstates are not welcoming or friendly to bicycles," I lamented. However, it was Sunday; the traffic was light. What was the worst that could happen?

I pedaled up the on ramp to I-55. I'd have only one mile to the exit for I-57. At the end of the ramp, just outside the flow of traffic, a man sat on the roadside, with a backpack and a cardboard sign with the word Louisiana printed in large letters. I braked to a stop and greeted him.

"I'd give you a ride if I had a bicycle built for two," I joked. He did not appear as disheveled as some hitchhikers I'd seen.

"My name's Joe," he said. "I'm surprised you even stopped."

"Why do you say that?"

"Most people are afraid of me. Folks are just afraid to pick up hitchhikers."

"Well, I'm not afraid of you. As a matter of fact, if you were to steal my bike, then I could go home." I nodded toward his sign. "Why Louisiana?"

"I had a job in Michigan and got laid off. There were no jobs available anywhere I looked, so I decided to hitchhike to the Gulf Coast to help with the cleanup from the BP oil spill. I heard they're looking for workers and paying well."

Joe went on to tell me his story. He had no job, money, or family. Drugs had put him in prison for many years. He made no excuses for his misdeeds, but acknowledged he had done wrong and deserved the prison sentence. While he was in prison, his wife had left him. And recently his son had committed suicide.

"I miss that boy so much. My life is a mess; and now here I am, sitting on the roadside, begging for rides." The poor fellow had tears slipping down his cheeks as he recounted his misbegotten past. He looked at me. "I'm honored you stopped to speak with me. But I have a question for you. Your face…you have such joy on your face. How is that possible? You're riding your bicycle across America alone, yet your face radiates joy."

"Joe," I said, "that joy comes from only one source, a personal relationship with Jesus Christ. That is the only source of joy."

"I used to have such high hopes for my future, then I messed it all up," said Joe.

"You can reclaim that, my friend. Jesus can put that joy on your face, too," I assured him.

"I want to show you something." He reached into his backpack and pulled out a writer's tablet. "At one time, I wanted to be an artist and a writer. Now, when I'm sitting under a bridge at night, I write my poetry and draw pictures." I paged through his drawings and skimmed over the poetry that expressed his innermost thoughts. How his talents had been squandered by bad choices!

"Tonight I'll write a poem about meeting the man with joy on his face," said Joe. I scribbled my address in his book and he promised to send me a copy of the poem.

I pulled out my wallet and handed a $20 bill to Joe. "I'm not asking for money," he said.

"Joe, I know you didn't ask, but I want to give you something. You have no money, and I can easily make it without this $20. I'm honored to be able to help you a little."

I pedaled away into the morning traffic heading east, but my thoughts stayed with Joe. I had purpose and meaning in my life. Joe was sitting by the roadside and sleeping under bridges, hoping only for a ride to Louisiana; and who knew what kind of life awaited him there? What had made the difference between our two lives?

I was born into a Christian home that started me on the right path. But I had made good choices and bad choices in life. All choices have consequences attached, and sometimes those consequences haunt folks for a lifetime. Joe's story was a sad example of the consequences of wrong choices. We all make wrong choices at times, and I knew that I could easily have been the one sitting on the roadside.

Joe wept as he mourned everything he'd lost; he looked at a solitary traveler and saw a joy he could not explain. The difference between our lives was that I had made one choice that has ramifications far above all the other choices I have ever made.

You have the same choice to make, my friend, and that decision is whether or not to allow Jesus into your life. This one good choice really can make up for a lifetime of bad choices. Choose wisely. The decision will affect you for all eternity.

I was the only biker on the interstate that Sunday. I suspect I was the only bicycle rider ever on that interstate, but it was also the only time Joe was going to be at that intersection. If I had followed my original route, we never would have met.

I pedaled furiously to the exit for I-57. The next eighteen miles on the shoulder of I-57 were the smoothest ride since the new road construction back in Colorado. This stretch was uneventful, although I was great entertainment for the dozens of eighteen-wheelers that rolled past me.

At Charleston, I exited I-57 and was reunited with Route 60. Several hours later, a long narrow bridge appeared in the distance. Bird Point sits at the confluence of the Mississippi and Ohio Rivers. Huge coal barges floated down the Mississippi as I pedaled over the high and narrow bridge.

I was just south of Cairo, Illinois, and the road made an abrupt right. Ahead rose another giant steel structure, the bridge across the Ohio River. As I approached the long ramp that would take me over the bridge, I spotted a highway sign indicating that US Highway 62 also crossed the river here. That same road runs within several hundred feet of my home in Berlin, Ohio.

The very road I was riding on held the promise of a journey home. As a boy, my world was defined by Route 241. My awareness of the world was determined by whatever distance I could pedal along that highway. When I was old enough to drive a vehicle, Routes 62 and 39 expanded my horizons. My world grew as I drove longer distances on those highways. I never really questioned where those routes started or ended; I just knew that they had always been a part of the world I called home.

One day, on a whim, I decided to follow Route 62 as far as it went in Ohio. I chased it all the way to the southern part of our state, to its merging with Route 68 and the point at which it sneaked into Kentucky. Now, years later and hundreds of miles away, in a place I'd never before visited—here was that same road that could take me home. I thought of Joe, homeless on the roadside. He had no route that could take him to a place called home.

Taking pleasure in this connection to my hometown, I pedaled up the long ramp leading to the narrow bridge. The highway here was two-lane and there was no shoulder; I rode with the traffic flow, but no one could pass me. It was a harrowing crossing. On the other side, another long ramp led away from the bridge. I rolled down that incline with great relief.

WELCOME TO KENTUCKY, the sign read. The Ohio River flowed on my right as I followed a series of earth levees and concrete floodwalls erected by the Army Corps of Engineers to prevent flooding.

The tagline on Kentucky's welcome sign read, UNBRIDLED SPIRIT. My own spirits were high. I was only one state removed from Ohio. I was so close to home, yet my journey was not over; my bike would still roll hundreds of miles as I turned south toward Florida.

At least, I had the promise of a road home. I wondered how far south Joe had traveled that day and what bridge he would call home that night.

CHAPTER 15

Biking the Bible Belt

A fter a day of navigating traffic on state routes and interstates, pedaling along a quaint little country road was relaxing. I was in farming country; corn fields lined the road and there was very little traffic to command my attention. I had an appointment that day, and my thoughts were on the amazing series of events that had brought me to this back road in rural Kentucky.

It all began on a mountainside in Massachusetts. God's plan undoubtedly existed long before that, but on that Sunday morning during my Appalachian Trail hike, I met God in a way that left me in tears, face down on the trail. He made a promise to me that day, and the sequence of events that followed brought me to this road bisecting the corn fields of Kentucky.

On my hike, I had relentlessly asked about the meaning of my life and whether God knew or even cared about what was happening to the world. That morning, God gave me a message that I was to include in the book I planned to write about my adventure.

I argued with Him. I wasn't the person to deliver such a message; it should come from a minister, not me. Frankly, I did not want to include it; people would think I was crazy, and my book wouldn't sell. *Put this message in your book, and I will get the book where I want it to go.* That was God's answer to my objections.

I realize that many folks raise an eyebrow when a person says he hears from God. And I admit, the idea does sound crazy if you don't know about God's plan for us.

Here are the basics of that plan: Humanity's sinful nature meant all of us were in deep trouble. God loves us; but He can't tolerate sin, so approaching God was impossible without a remedy for the sin problem. God provided that remedy, sending His son Jesus to die as a sacrifice for the sins of the world. On the cross, Jesus took all our nasty, bad stuff on Himself and paid the price for our sins.

Here's the really good part. By believing in Jesus and trusting this great sacrifice, we are saved. Jesus' death was our redemption, our rescue from the punishment for our sins. The door is now opened for a relationship with God. When we realize the hopelessness of our sinful condition and accept the sacrifice made for us, the Holy Spirit comes and dwells within us! A part of God lives in us. That is quite incredible.

Now back to the question as to how we hear from God. God certainly hears from us; most folks reading this would probably say that they pray. But I've heard Christians say, "Yes, I pray, but I hear nothing back."

I believe there are many ways God speaks to us, but I'd like to focus on two. Let's use examples from marriage.

Suppose your spouse passed away and left you written instructions on how to do everything from laundry to fixing a leaky faucet. It would then be foolish for you to complain about not being able to do the laundry if you haven't read the instructions. The Bible is the written guide that God gave us. It is the Creator's direct word to us, His creation. You will learn to know Him by reading the Bible.

That written guide tells us that the Spirit of God living within us will teach us and lead us into truth. The more you get to know God, the more His Spirit teaches and guides you. Spouses often know each other so well that they each know what the other is thinking without any words being spoken. That knowing comes from much communication. On a greater spiritual level, that's what happens as we learn to know God; we read His Word, we talk to Him in prayer, and God's Spirit living in us leads and speaks to us.

I know this sounds impossible and preposterous to many people, but you cannot understand and experience this until you take that first step and believe in God's plan—believe in what Jesus did for us sinful humans.

And if you are a Christian but are missing out on the joy of dialogue with the Holy Spirit, I urge you to read your Bible with a new zeal and a desire for God to reveal Himself to you. It can happen, and it will happen.

If I were in the pulpit instead of sitting at a keyboard and writing this book, we would now have an invitation and lift an offering.

I chose to believe God when He said he would get *Hiking Through* wherever He wanted it to go. He was in charge of the sales department and I just hung on for the ride.

Shortly before leaving on my bicycle journey, I received an email from a major Christian publishing house stating their interest in purchasing the rights to my book. I'd always heard that it was virtually impossible for an unknown author to be picked up by the established, traditional publishers. That would be the equivalent of a high school baseball player being picked up by a major league team without going through all the training camps and the minor leagues. However, with God all things are possible.

The publishing house wanted to release the book all across America, making it available in far more places than it already was. While the offer was exciting, I was unsure if I wanted to relinquish the rights to my book. I had many unanswered questions, and I prayed for wisdom and guidance in my decision.

The publisher offered me a contract and gave me a phone number for the editor who would be working with me. This decision had, of course, been on my mind while I biked; and on the night I was in Sikeston, Missouri, I decided to call the editor to introduce myself. The publisher was headquartered in Michigan, and I assumed my new editor also lived there.

We introduced ourselves to each other and then chatted about my bicycle trip. "I'm in Sikeston, Missouri, tonight. Tomorrow I'll be heading over to Paducah, Kentucky, and then south to Florida."

"I live in Paducah!" said the editor. "Our company is in Michigan, but I work out of my home here in Kentucky. Let's get together tomorrow night and discuss any questions you might have."

I was astounded. What were the chances of that happening? What if I had waited just a few more days to call? What if my editor had lived anywhere else but the town that was my destination for the next day? After the phone call, I fell to my knees in thankful adoration.

God was still in control and carrying out His promise to take *Hiking Through* exactly where He wanted it to go.

My editor told me that both state routes leading into Paducah were busy highways with no shoulder for bicycles, and she gave me directions that followed small country roads instead. She and her husband, it turned out, also loved bicycling; they rode twenty miles out into the country to meet me and escort me through the corn fields into Paducah.

I checked into my room and we made plans to meet for dinner that evening. I had pushed my bike into the motel lobby just before a cloudburst drenched the streets. The front desk clerk was curious about my cross-country ride, but I wanted to do my laundry and prepare for my meeting that night, so I promised her I'd stop back later and explain my purpose in riding across America.

Over a delicious barbeque meal, my editor and I discussed the sale of my book and my questions were answered. It almost felt as though I were selling one of my children, but I knew it was the right thing to do. God apparently had plans, and so I agreed to sell the rights to *Hiking Through.*

I did go back to the front desk clerk to tell her about my ride. When she realized I was a Christian and I related some of my stories about what God was revealing on my journey, I saw her face come alive with excitement. Then she told me her own story.

"I am a single mom with a teenage son and, with the help of my parents, I'm just managing to survive financially. I recently became a Christian, and then my prayer was that my son would also get saved.

"I bought a pair of shoes for my son, but they were too tight. So we needed to exchange them. A Christian youth convention was taking place a number of miles from our house, and my son had been invited and wanted to attend. I thought it would be great for him to go, but there was no money for gas. I had just enough gas to get to the shoe store and back. We exchanged the shoes for a larger size and were about to leave when the clerk said, 'Wait, I owe you money. You get a $10 refund.'

"I now had money for gas, so I drove my son to the youth meeting; and later that evening, he responded to an invitation to accept Christ. Can you imagine that? My son got saved because his shoes were too tight!"

Yes, of course I could imagine that. I was quite aware that God moved in mysterious ways. I was still thinking about how God had directed me earlier that morning to a meeting with Joe on the side of the interstate.

I had been so blessed to be able to give Joe a small amount of money. God loves a cheerful giver, we are told; and I was never so happy to give a twenty away, giving no thought to getting any kind of monetary blessings from my gesture. It should not have surprised me that God also blesses cheerful givers, yet I would be very surprised the following day.

Scattered storm clouds still scurried overhead as I navigated my way out of Paducah the next morning. Heading south on Route 68 near Sharpe, Kentucky, I was intrigued by The Apple Valley Hillbilly Gardens and Toyland Museum. The sign said Sorry We're Open, and I admired the unconventional humor. The place is quite an attraction. Perhaps *distraction* would be a better description.

The owner is an artist turning everyday junk into eclectic objects of art. Lawn mowers hung from trees. A bicycle had been cut in half and welded to a lawn mower creating a riding mower of sorts. A sign above an open commode showed folks where to place gossip.

Enjoying my stroll through the artist's ingenious creations, I chuckled at a thought. If all his creations were left on the ground, this would surely be called a junkyard. With a little creative flair, this junk now had value. In reality, I was strolling through an elevated junk pile. To my disappointment, though, there was no stash of old comic books.

This was my only full day in Kentucky, and for most of the day my bike rolled through rural areas. Besides my departure city of Paducah, only three towns appeared along my route. I felt right at home in the first town. The sign at the town line said, Welcome To Benton. My childhood hometown of Benton, Ohio, has several hundred friendly people; Benton, Kentucky, has over 4,000. Murray, at slightly over 17,000 residents, was home to Murray State University. Hazel was the last small town I pedaled through before entering Tennessee. Only a few more than 400 folks call Hazel home.

It did pay to visit Hazel. I was just leaving a service station where I had stopped for a cold beverage. Ahead, the Tennessee state line appeared. Another state behind me!

Then something else caught my eye, a silver blur on the roadside as my wheels rolled by. I was fairly certain I'd also caught sight of some money attached to the silver. The day had already yielded a decent take of roadside spoils, and my coffers had been enlarged by nearly fifty cents. I turned around.

Collecting dust beside the road was a silver money clip. Its surface showed some wear, undoubtedly from its time here on the roadside; and it gripped what appeared to be several dollars. I shoved it into my pocket, believing I had increased my net worth by about $3. Hooray for Hazel. I guessed the larger value of my find was in the clip itself; it was solid silver.

I was soon in Tennessee and one state closer to my journey's end. In two days, my cousin from Sarasota, Florida, would meet me in southern Tennessee and ride with me through Alabama, Georgia, and part of Florida. Elated at entering another state, I quickly forgot the silver loot in my pocket.

In downtown Paris I encountered a street vendor selling hot dogs. Finding a good hot dog ranks high on my "pleasurable events" list, right up there with finding money. The hot dog was great, and my conversation with the street vendor was most productive. He gave me directions to a motel with a good restaurant adjacent. I concluded my day with an hour's nap in the tub, submerged in ever-cooling water. The Italian meal next door was delicious, as promised, and I was quite happy and contented as I slipped under the covers.

"That money clip!" I almost shouted. I had forgotten to count the money Hazel had given me. I grabbed my pants from the floor, rummaged through the pockets, and pulled out the clip. The wad of money was tightly packed into its silver sheath. I was correct about one thing. There were three ones. I peeled those away and revealed a few twenties. Inside the twenties, seven Ben Franklins had convened. For those not sure where Ben Franklin's visage appears, it's at the center of one hundred dollar bills. My hands were shaking as I counted.

Instantaneously, I remembered the $20 I had handed Joe. Yesterday morning, I'd given a homeless man a single twenty, knowing he could never repay me. What had not occurred to me at the time was that God is only too happy to bless a cheerful giver. I had given a twenty and received over $700 back. You can't out-give God. Hmmm…maybe I should have given the man $40.

The following day, I called the local police department to see if anyone had reported losing such a large amount of money. The phone line was busy. I tried to call several businesses in the area where I found the loot, but had no success. I do believe God intended it for me.

Since then, I've had several folks proclaim their joy and gratitude to me for finding their money. If you're thinking of claiming this wad, describe the design of the money clip, and the money is yours. Thus far, no one has come close to doing that.

Leaving Paris early the next morning, I glimpsed a vignette of quiet patriotism. In front of the courthouse, a man was raising an American flag. His hat was off, held respectfully in one hand. He never saw me silently gliding by.

There are many things going wrong in this country, but there is also so much good. I thought of the many freedoms we still enjoy. I'd traveled almost 4,000 miles, and no policeman had stopped me or challenged my passage; I rode freely from town to town, state to state. Churches openly advertise their services. The majority of Americans are still decent, law-abiding citizens. Strangers showed me many kindnesses. I always parked my bike and left it unsecured, and no one ever bothered it.

I will admit, however, the habit of leaving my bike unattended now produced an uneasy feeling. That money clip and its contents rode at the bottom of my pannier. Can you imagine the surprise of any bandit absconding with my bicycle and discovering the bounty hidden deep within my pannier?

I don't know where the proverbial Bible Belt starts or stops, but the abundance of churches convinced me that I was riding somewhere along the buckle. Church signs of all shapes and sizes and construction broadcast clever messages, short one-line sermons. Although I was amused at many of the witticisms, sometimes a message spoke to me so directly that I cringed. The August weather was hot, and the signs capitalized on that. OUR CHURCH IS PRAYER CONDITIONED, one read. THE TEMPERATURE IN HELL NEVER CHANGES, warned another. Whether serious or lighthearted, all the signs were posted with one intention—to win the lost and exhort everyone to love his neighbor as himself.

Outside Camden, Tennessee, a lady was struggling to change a flat tire.

"Go help that lady," breathed the Spirit.

"No, I don't think so," replied my human nature. She was on the other side of the highway, across four lanes of traffic. "Someone in the other lane can help."

"Do you see anyone stopping?"

"No, but there's a lot of traffic, and we're in the Bible Belt. With all those church signs proclaiming the love of God, surely someone will help her."

But the prodding would not cease.

"Oh, all right, I'll do it."

I pushed my bike across the grass median and the other two lanes and approached her disabled vehicle. She was bent over, making a valiant effort to remove the deflated tire.

"Good morning—can I help you change that tire?"

She screamed and jumped in fright. She was so absorbed in her task that she hadn't seen me arrive.

"Yes, I sure could use help. I've been stranded here for two hours. You're the first person to stop. I've been trying to pry this wheel cover off. It just won't come off."

"Let me take a look." I took a look. "I don't mean to be rude, but you could keep prying away there all day and never get it off. You have your pry bar on the rim. The strongest man in the world couldn't pry off that rim."

She looked at me with a sheepish grin when I popped the wheel cover with one quick flick. Through laughter and tears she recounted how she had called everyone she could think of to help her, but no one could come to her aid until later in the morning. And although we were on a busy highway, no one had stopped. "So I decided to just change it myself. If you hadn't shown up, I'd probably be here all day."

After the new tire was on, I turned to leave. She shoved a twenty dollar bill into my hand.

"Oh no, I don't want your money." She insisted I take it. Two days before, I had given a homeless man twenty dollars; and now money I didn't need or deserve was coming my way.

I pushed my bike back across the median strip and continued my journey. Everything at once seemed lighter and brighter. The sun was shining, my spirit was lifted, and the journey was light. It is a good thing to help other folks. How often do we see a need and think that someone else will fill it? Perhaps if it has been revealed to us, then it is our duty to act on it. Money can't buy the peace and joy that fills you when you listen to that prompting from the Holy Spirit.

By noon I had crossed over I-40. Midway between Nashville and Memphis on Route 641, I changed my course. My cousin Marvin would be meeting me in Pulaski, Tennessee, the following evening, so I looked for a route that would take me farther southeast. Judging from the map, I'd be doing a backcountry trek through small towns with no lodging.

At a convenience store, several local ladies assured me there was a small inn located in downtown Linden. I set that town as my destination for the day. This would also set me up to reach Pulaski the following day.

The 1,000 residents of Linden have undertaken a complete makeover of their downtown. This area is famous for good hunting and fishing and spectacular scenery. Local artists are involved in the renaissance, and their talents are visible on murals throughout the downtown.

The Commodore Hotel Linden on East Main Street was just completing a major overhaul. This historic inn was my destination, but when I walked in, the price quoted to me apparently covered the entire cost of remodeling my room.

"Will I get the deed to your building, too?" I joked. They took my humor in the same spirit it was given, so I put on my saddest tired face and told them about my hard day biking through the rugged Tennessee countryside. The truth was, my choices were limited. The next town was Hohenwald, another twenty hilly, winding miles away. I really had no other choice but to stay here. "I'm writing a book about my journey. Perhaps I could make you famous by including you in my book." A deal was struck. At about half the previously quoted price, I could have a room; and in return, I would mention them in my upcoming masterpiece.

To my new friends at the Commodore Hotel Linden, our contractual obligations have been fulfilled. Deal done. Finished. Lovely inn, friendly reception, beautiful rooms, no elevator, had to carry my bicycle up two flights of stairs. Neat town. Readers, mention this book and get a discount. (Maybe that last statement wasn't part of the deal?)

Leaving the Commodore the following morning, I noticed something I had missed the previous day. Hanging over the front entrance was a plastic bag filled with water. I had seen that before somewhere. Yes, I remember, back in Newport, Oregon, while waiting for Andy at the Red Door Deli. The water bag at the Commodore, however, had one additional ingredient. A shiny penny lay at the bottom of the bulging bag.

"Does it really work?" I asked a maintenance man working on repairs at the front door. He assured me it did. The yellow jackets see the penny and think it's another yellow jacket staring back at them. They'll buzz about for a long time bumping up against that bag; and in their confusion, they forget they were planning to check into the Commodore and eventually buzz off.

My ride to Hohenwald was beautiful, if somewhat harrowing. The route was used heavily by truck traffic, and the lack of shoulders forced me out on the road to compete for riding space.

One mile outside of Hohenwald, I took a break at a service station. A local truck driver and I struck up a conversation. From his trucking experience, he recognized the name of my hometown.

"You're from Amish Country, then," he said. "We have an Amish community just east of here, over towards Summertown."

"What's the best way to get to Pulaski?" I wondered.

"Take 20 over to Summertown, then 43 will take you all the way down to Lawrenceburg where you'll intersect Route 64 heading east to Pulaski. That's a very busy road, though; you better be real careful. Lots of trucks use that route, and you'll probably encounter some Amish buggies from here to Lawrenceburg."

The truck driver chuckled as he related a story about a local Amish man who used his tractor for transportation. "Those Amish folks, they are quite ingenious, you know. That man replaced the tractor's gear ratio and transmission with a pickup truck's transmission, and he'd zip around town at pretty good speeds. One day he got stopped and cited for not having a seatbelt on his ride."

Apparently the man is no longer riding about at excessive speeds. I suppose both the lawman and the truck driver thought the citation was what put the kibosh on the speedster. I wondered, though, if a higher authority behind the scenes might have had some input in the decision. But I kept that thought to myself.

Back on the road again, I heard a familiar sound, the clip-clop of a horse's hooves on pavement. If I closed my eyes, I might have believed I was back home. If I closed my eyes, I would also wreck my bike.

The open buggy was clip-clopping toward me. An older man and his wife were heading into town. I wanted to stop, but there was too much traffic. Instead, I yelled a Pennsylvania Dutch greeting across the road as we passed. The poor man almost fell out of his hack when he heard the biker with the fancy blue and white helmet and bright racing shirt speaking his language.

Several miles later, I arrived at Yoder's Homestead Market, a small country store. I surprised the young Amish girl at the front counter with another Pennsylvania Dutch greeting and then enjoyed a large deli sandwich. Browsing through the market, I inquired where they bought the meats and cheeses on display at their counter.

"We get delivery from Troyer's Cheese once a week," the girl replied. Small world, I thought. Troyer's Cheese is located in Berlin, Ohio, where I live.

By the time I rolled into Summertown, my ice cream gauge had fallen to an alarmingly low level. The situation was rectified at a small grocery store. While I ate my ice cream and chatted with the clerk, her son entered the store, obviously agitated. He told his mom that a high school classmate had been shot and killed the previous evening in Lawrenceburg, in an argument about his girlfriend. What a sad ending to a young life.

I recalled another sad ending for a young friend of mine. We took that fateful bike ride on Labor Day weekend back in 1966. My cousin from Florida had been the third rider that night. He and

I had been boys then, having fun together on our bicycles. After the accident, we parked our bikes and never rode together again. Now we were going to bike together once more. Just slightly older boys, still trying to have fun.

We were meeting at the motel in Pulaski. Just before eleven o'clock that night, my phone rang; my cousin had arrived. I walked over to his room to greet him and go over plans for our ride the next day. I had ridden through ten states in fifty-four days. Tomorrow, Marv would dispatch with his first state and begin his second, all within just a few hours. We'd start here in Tennessee, but Alabama was only thirty miles away.

Walking back to my room, I realized it was September 1, 2010. Precisely forty-four years ago, to the day and hour, the three of us had rolled out the long lane together for a moonlight bike ride.

Dear God, are You thinking what I'm thinking? You wouldn't dare; You couldn't. You didn't bring us together to wipe another one of us off the map, did You? I know that sounds silly and maybe juvenile and certainly not theologically correct, but I will admit I was a little shaken by the coincidence. The thought of Marvin and I meeting again for a bike ride, exactly forty-four years after that accident...

I felt safe; I was convinced I was where God wanted me to be. But was Marvin where God wanted him to be? I knew he was prepared spiritually, should the worst occur. How would I ever explain if anything happened? I do not believe in coincidence; I believe God's hand is in the timing of our lives. But why now, why on September 1?

One thing did worry me, though. I can be somewhat daring, but Marv is even more of a risk-taker than I am. We had hiked together, and at places where my fear of cliff edges kicked in and common sense prevailed, my cousin's fear had not even wakened to the danger.

Marv's wife Rita assumed I knew what I was doing and would look out for her husband; but knowing his boldness, I expected some nerve-racking miles ahead.

CHAPTER 16

Kudzu, Cotton Fields, and Canines

"So, does that oversized launching pad really protect your behind?"

Every time I'd glanced in my mirror that morning, a rider had been on my tail. I was no longer biking solo, and I was amazed how the presence of one other person changed my journey.

Marv and I had stopped to admire the panorama of cotton fields off in the distance. I'd been studying his big, plush bike seat all morning. Back in Fallon, Nevada, I'd seen the same seat when I was shopping for more comfort; however, at that time I was riding on a new seat I had just purchased in San Francisco for $60, and I doubted that I'd get more comfort from one priced far below what I had already paid.

"I bought this at Wal-Mart for $24, and it seems comfortable," replied my cousin.

I was still alternating my bike seats every few days in an effort to minimize back-end blues. After all the trouble I'd gone through trying to find comfort for my discomfort, could the solution really be as simple as a cheap, cushioned granny seat?

Thirty miles into our morning we arrived in Ardmore, Alabama. At a gas station, I spotted an air pump and decided it was probably time to check my tire pressure. I'd given no thought to that preventive maintenance since Colorado. My laying on of hands and a little prayer each morning had kept my bike rolling along trouble-free. Several pounds of pressure had indeed escaped somewhere back in the plains, so I added a few pounds of Alabama air.

Route 53 took us south toward Route 431, the highway we planned to take all the way to Columbus, Georgia. Our course led through one of Alabama's largest cities, Huntsville. Passage through this urban region was a harrowing experience for my riding partner on his first day on the highway. When we had biked together in adventurous boyhood, the two of us had owned the quiet country roads; now constant vigilance was necessary. Thousands of cars and trucks rushed by us, only a few feet from our unprotected bikes and bodies.

We cautiously maneuvered our way through busy city streets and at last reached 431 on the eastern side of town. The city quickly disappeared behind us, giving way to the rolling Alabama farming country. Although now free of the heavy traffic, we had a new concern; in this rural area, motels were few and far between.

A store clerk told us of a new motel in Hampton Cove. On the road again, we were relieved to spot a billboard confirming that information. Stopping at Hampton Cove would shorten our day to only fifty-four miles; but it was hot and muggy, and if we bypassed this motel we would be forced to pedal another thirty miles to Guntersville. Several restaurants and a Wal-Mart near the new motel sealed our decision; we ended our day early in Hampton Cove.

Later that evening, I replaced my expensive instrument of torture with a new $24 comfort station I purchased at Wal-Mart. The new seat was big, it was wide, it was high. It was unsightly, but I was desperate.

After several adjustments the next morning, I went sailing along atop my new perch. And I was comfortable. Could it really be true that 4,000 miles of backside distress were finally behind me?

Alabama was a surprise. I'd always thought of the state as flat and covered with cotton fields. Instead, the rolling green country-side, small farms, and grazing cattle reminded me of home. It was a very scenic ride. The cotton fields were there, too, interspersed with the green pastures; and they reminded me that this was not home.

The cotton looked ready to harvest, like fluffy white popcorn growing on low bushes. I've traveled quite a bit, but these were the first cotton fields I'd ever seen. We stopped at one field and invited ourselves in for a closer look. The weevil was once cotton's most feared pest; now, destruction is visited upon cotton plants by bicycle riders who pull, pry, and dissect the innermost workings of a cotton boll. I was fascinated by the plant and how important it is to our lives today. Bath towels, robes, denim jeans, and even coffee filters result from these fluffy white mounds.

Since the previous day's ride was relatively short, we wanted to get in a longer day. Towns were not spaced to our liking, though, and lodging was difficult to find. We had eighty miles behind us when a large hill loomed ahead. I was riding in luxury on my high foam chair, but my legs were extremely tired. Marv's muscles had even less conditioning and he was suffering greatly. We dismounted and slowly pushed our bikes upward.

A Good Samaritan passed and then pulled off the road just ahead of us.

"Hey, fellows, do you need a lift somewhere?" He assumed that we were pushing our rides because we had mechanical difficulties. We explained that it was body mechanics that had caused us to dismount.

I had noticed the bike rack attached to the rear of his vehicle. In our conversation about my ride across America, we discovered that he was an avid rider and very knowledgeable about the area. I asked about the road conditions we would encounter through the rest of Alabama.

"This road is four-lane and very busy, and you'll have even heavier traffic tomorrow as you go farther south. Auburn University has a football game, and the people around here are rabid fans." Our goal for the following evening was the town of Opelika, next door to Auburn. He advised us to rethink that goal. "Those motel rooms will all be taken by fans attending the game."

I commented on the poor and sometimes nonexistent road shoulders we had encountered that afternoon. The gentleman was well versed on biking law in Alabama and informed us that motorists were required to give bicyclists a three-foot zone of highway in which to ride. This was the wrong thing to tell my biking partner. He had no fear of man or beast, and so he embraced that law and claimed the last three feet of highway as his personal space.

"I have a right to it, and I'll use it," said the voice riding behind me. "I can't keep my bike on an eight-inch shoulder like you do. You've had 4,000 miles of practice. I'll just use my three feet."

I was now certain of it; Marv would be run over by some monster truck, a massive RV, or maybe even a little VW bug. But it was going to happen, no doubt about it. I wondered if he remembered what weekend this was. I cast supplications, begging, and pleas for safety over my shoulder, all while rehearsing my conversation with his spouse when the inevitable happened. "But he was within his three-foot zone," I could add when telling the story.

We pedaled ninety-three miles that second day and stayed at the first place we found, just outside Saks, Alabama. Once in our room, Marv refused to leave. The day had completely exhausted the poor man. We had Chinese food delivered, and my cousin did not move far from his three feet of safety on his mattress. His last words before passing out were, "I didn't think it would be this difficult."

The following day we were entertained by revelers heading toward the Auburn football game. Hundreds of vehicles, with banners and flags waving, headed down Route 431. At a grocery store, the clerks advised us to stop in Roanoke for the night. No place between Roanoke and Auburn would have rooms available, they predicted. It was a short fifty-five-mile day through the Talladega National Forest to our motel in Roanoke.

The motel was called the Key West Inn. I took this as a good omen, since Key West was my hoped-for destination. At the front desk, we were given directions to a restaurant rated highly by the local folks. It was a barbeque joint that did not disappoint. As we walked back to our motel, a sign in the shape of a large ice cream cone screamed for our attention. We decided that another 500 calories might be just what our bodies needed.

Among the boards listing descriptions of various ice cream indulgences, a sign propped against the window read, TRUST IN THE LORD WITH ALL YOUR HEART AND LEAN NOT ON YOUR OWN UNDERSTANDING. PROVERBS 3:5. The Scripture summoned up good memories. My dad had taught his children that verse long ago and quoted it often to his family over the years.

The small sign also reminded me of all the church signs I'd been reading as I pedaled along. In Paris, Tennessee, one sign proclaimed, CHILDREN WILL NOT LISTEN TO YOUR ADVICE AND IGNORE YOUR EXAMPLE. Another in Hohenwald announced, WIN A NEW HOUSE, FREE CHANCES AT EVERY SERVICE. And one I had spotted earlier that day read, CHURCH ATTENDANCE IS NOT AN ELEVATOR TO HEAVEN.

Now here in Roanoke an ice cream shop posted Bible verses. I admit, I wondered about the sincerity of the proprietor's intentions. A stocky man inside shouted out a friendly greeting. "What can I do for you?"

Remembering my dad's King James quote, I replied, "In all thy ways acknowledge Him, and He will direct thy paths, Proverbs 3:6."

He laughed and replied, "That's on the other side of the sign."

"I like the sign," I said. "I've noticed there are many churches in this part of Alabama; I suppose I'm riding along the Bible belt?"

That opened our conversation, and any doubts I had about the man's sincerity vanished.

"I'm a pastor here in Roanoke. I believe we're on this earth to help other folks," he explained. I told him about my ride and some of the desperate folks I had met. He also had a story to tell about helping someone in need.

"Several years ago, a fellow came through here on a bicycle, pulling a cart. His dog sat in the cart, along with all the man's belongings. The fellow was looking for work, so I put him up in my basement for several days and gave him odd jobs around the church."

One of the parishioners had an RV, and he parked that behind the church and allowed the man to stay there. He was still living in the RV, several years later. Now he works around the church and just recently committed his life to Christ.

"We never pushed him or made demands of him," said the pastor ice cream man. "We just loved him. Finally one Sunday he responded to an invitation, and his tears showed true repentance."

What an example of the church reaching out to help someone in hardship! Perhaps I had been too cynical about the ineffectiveness of those church signs and folks not responding to a traveler in trouble. All that is necessary is that one person respond—the person to whom the need is revealed.

Something was reaching out to me. Vine runners cascaded down over road banks and green tentacles stretched toward the highway and tried to snag my leg.

At the 1886 Philadelphia Exposition, Japan gifted America with the kudzu vine. Kudzu has the ability to grow at an incredible rate, up to sixty feet per year. During the Depression of the 1930s, the Soil Conservation Corps hired hundreds of men to plant kudzu in areas where erosion was a problem. The plan worked like a charm.

As a matter of fact, the planting was too successful. The kudzu spread over those troublesome, washed-out areas and then kept on growing. Now the plant is marching across the South like an army, growing over anything in its path. Kudzu overwhelms entire forests, and trees and bushes soon die when deprived of sunlight. All over the South, interesting green shapes rise from the landscape as kudzu encases anything in its path, including abandoned cars and even houses.

To date, the vine has swept over 7 million acres and is expanding its conquests at the rate of 150,000 acres a year. Almost indestructible, the plant is only inhibited for a short time by chemicals; then it roars back to life. Some cities have sent goats and llamas to the battlefront to fight the advancing green legions.

Kudzu is a fair-weather vine and does not thrive in cold climates, so it dines only on the South. Thank you, Japan.

"What's been your experience with dogs?" My cousin had posed that question to me the night before.

Although I do like dogs as family pets and companions, I'm always fearful of canine encounters as I pedal along. A little Chihuahua bark can bring me out of the saddle in a second and set me to pedaling furiously. "I've been very fortunate so far," I told Marv. "Several dogs back in California gave chase, but they didn't catch me. Not much else has happened. Kentucky is supposedly the worst state for dogs on the loose, but none bothered me."

"I have no fear of dogs, never have," replied Marv. That didn't surprise me much; he had no fear of high cliff edges or barreling eighteen wheelers. The very next day, the intrepid traveler would be tested.

The morning was gorgeous in rural Alabama. Cattle roamed in green pastures. Lakes reflected clouds in blue sky. The rolling terrain was not too difficult, and I was enjoying the ride.

Then I spotted trouble ahead.

A pack of three dogs ran through the field next to us; their gait and the tilt of their heads told me immediately that they were out looking for trouble. These were not house pets; they were real beasts. One large mixed breed that showed traits of a shepherd was in the lead; two other mongrels followed him.

Marv was several hundred feet behind me. So, he's not afraid of dogs; might this encounter change his mind?

The Fearless One would have to fend for himself. I did a quick mental triangulation, calculating my position, the spot at which the dogs and my bicycle would probably intersect, and the point farther down the road where I believed I would be safe.

The lead dog spotted me. His beast brain spent no time calculating. An instinct for the chase kicked in, he gave a howl, and all three beasts did a turnabout. The race was on.

Man, could those dogs run; but propelling my bike across 4,000-plus miles had also given me spectacular leg muscles. I pointed to the field and yelled *"Dogs!"* and pedaled like a madman.

The dogs squeezed and wriggled through the board fence, delayed just long enough that I managed to get ahead of them. Howling with delight, they chased me down the road. The big shepherd led the way while the other two long-eared hounds tore after him. I admired their tenacity, but I had such a head of steam that I outdistanced them.

But what about my cousin? *He's going to be a sitting duck*, I thought. I was convinced he would soon be sacrificing body parts to the marauders.

A bloodcurdling scream nearly rocked me off my bike. The dogs had been concentrating on their prey and had not seen Marv charging them from behind. His scream scared the livin' daylights out of the pack.

Fear brings two options, fight or flight. While the mongrels were willing to fight with me, the wrath of the shrieking unknown had taken them by surprise and they chose flight. Ears flapping, tails extending straight out behind, the pack fled up the bank and scrambled back through the board fence to the safety of the pasture. The pursuers had become the pursued and turned tail in fear of impending doom.

I have witnessed it with my own eyes…and ears. My cousin truly has no fear of dogs.

"What a harmless little bunch of cowards," he scoffed as we rode on, all body parts intact.

In the middle of the afternoon, we crossed the bridge spanning the Chattahoochee River. Halfway across the bridge, a sign welcomed us to Georgia. Even more exciting was the posting beneath that sign, a notice that we were entering the Eastern Time Zone. I had finally returned to "home" time. I'd pedaled in four time zones in my journey across America and had returned all three hours that had been granted me on my flight to Seattle.

We had covered seventy-three miles when we decided to stop in Columbus. A plenitude of restaurants and motels in the area made that an easy decision. We also needed to plan our route through this next state. Route 431 had taken us through Alabama and then turned into Route 280 as we entered Georgia. Our plan was to pedal through the southwestern corner of Georgia on a route that would usher us into Florida somewhere east of Tallahassee.

Columbus is home to Fort Benning, and I marveled at the size of this complex. Covering over 182,000 acres, this US Army post supports over 120,000 active and retired military folks and many civilians who also work and live on the base. We passed several exits leading into Fort Benning, and I spotted an enemy army creeping along the outside perimeter of the post. Even the mightiest military in the world was not immune to attack by the menacing kudzu.

All across America, I observed crops flourishing in areas where the climate and growing conditions are most ideal for those particular plants. The fragrant lavender fields in Washington, myrtle in Oregon, giant redwoods in the coastal fogs, and even dusty tumbleweeds thrive in settings most conducive to their growth. I suppose we could also include marijuana on that list; that crop also grows where the climate nourishes it.

In Georgia, we rode through the countryside in awe of stately pecan trees reaching heights of 75 to 100 feet. Groves cover thousands of acres, and Georgia is the leading producer of pecans in the United States. Roadside stands selling the produce dot the countryside.

At the retail and gift shop of one large distributor, I was lured in by a sign boasting of the best pecan pie in the world. I purchased a hot dog and root beer for my main course and a small pecan pie for dessert, and then took my treats to one of the inviting chairs on the long front porch.

A number of workers also sat there, obviously on break. I was curious; and in answer to my questions, they explained, in a deep southern drawl, the pecan harvesting and shipping process. This was a large distributor, and the fruit was shipped out by semi loads. (Yes, the pecan is technically a fruit.)

They, in turn, were curious about my ride. "How far are you riding?" one asked.

"All the way to Key West, Florida," I replied. Exclamations of incredulity came from the crowd.

"That's over 500 miles away!" exclaimed one worker. "You've got to be crazy." What I welcomed as only a short ride to my destination seemed like an impossible distance to them.

"I've ridden from the northwest corner of Washington State, over 4,000 miles, to get here. Key West is just around the corner."

"Are you out of your mind? Are you nuts?" shouted my audience.

"Wait a minute, guys. You all work in a pecan warehouse, and you're calling me nuts?"

Our conversation also caught the attention of passersby. One lady approached and asked about my ride and examined my bicycle.

"My son loves to ride bicycle, too," she said. "We came down to Fort Benning to see him today. He just returned from two years in Iraq." The relief in her face was evident as she spoke of the worrying and praying she had done while her son was overseas. "I realize how fortunate I am to have him back. Many other moms across America weren't so fortunate."

Our break was soon over. Even being generous, I could give the pecan pie only an average rating. I should have told my new friends to visit Amish Country if they wanted great pecan pie.

"Well, fellows, I'd better head for Key West."

As Marv and I pedaled out of the gravel lot, I heard laughter from the porch and snippets of comments about my sanity. "He's crazy." "He's out of his mind."

Out on the highway, we went from groves to grooves. The Georgia Department of Highways apparently was obsessed with its shoulder grinder. I had ridden before through areas where the road shoulders were mutilated by grooving. This practice is meant as a safety measure, to wake up drifting drivers and signal that a correction is needed immediately.

For a bicycle rider, though, these stretches turn hostile and tortuous. Shallow grooves can sometimes be tolerated; they might, perhaps, even provide a gentle massage for a tired body. But a deeply grooved shoulder sends jolts reverberating like an electric shock through every muscle. Our route through Dawson, Albany, and Thomasville was filled with this Georgia roadside insanity. I was convinced that each operator working the grinder had used his own discretion on depth and length of the irritating obstacles, and it seemed obvious that most of those same operators must have been hired from the coal fields and believed they were strip mining the shoulders in search of minerals.

In some areas, the machine operator had been generous and left eight inches of shoulder unmarred. I threaded my bike along this small area, but Marv insisted he could not contain his rig to such a small piece of real estate. His riding sphere included every inch of the three feet of highway legally open to him. Miraculously, we managed sixty-five miles in spite of Georgia giving us the cold shoulder.

When we arrived in Thomasville and checked in at the Day's Inn Motel, my curiosity finally got the better of me. The clerk was of Indian descent. All across America I had found this to be the case; many Subways and Dunkin Donuts and most of the places where I'd found lodging were owned by immigrants from India.

I asked the young clerk for confirmation of my observations, and he freely shared his family's story. His father had immigrated years ago; he had little money but was determined to pursue the American dream of business ownership. The young man told me about the network of Indian families who help each other realize this dream. "We believe it's possible for anyone in America to succeed if they really try," he said.

It was good to hear that there are still folks who believe in the American spirit of hard work and success. While many Americans lament the lack of jobs, folks from other countries who experience a true dearth of opportunity are able to see potential all across this land.

The jarring road conditions were not the only thing troubling me. All day I had been thinking about an anniversary. We often measure time by the number of years that have passed since a certain event. Birthdays measure the time spent on earth. Wedding anniversaries are a good thing to celebrate. These dates commemorate events that have had an impact on our lives. Anniversaries gauge progress in our lives.

That day in Georgia was the fourth anniversary of my wife's death. My life had changed in so many ways since that sad evening four years ago. I saw a church sign in Alabama that advised, WHEN LIFE KNOCKS YOU TO YOUR KNEES, YOU ARE IN THE PERFECT POSITION TO PRAY. Only those who have lost a spouse, a parent, or a child can understand the harshness, the abruptness of such a separation. After such a loss, the only place to start the healing process is on your knees.

On the night of Mary's funeral service, after everyone had gone and I was alone, I did just that; I fell on my knees by my bedside and, between sobs, prayed for guidance. A familiar verse (thanks, Dad) kept coming to me. "In all thy ways acknowledge Him, and He will direct thy paths." I chose to believe this, and my faith in that promise completely changed my life. I was led to retire from a great job I enjoyed and take a 2,176-mile journey in the wilderness. This bicycle ride across America was also a result of my trust in God's direction. Anyone who thinks that following God is boring and restrictive is missing out on a fulfilling life; it's a great adventure.

As I pedaled through Georgia on September 7, I reflected on the many ways my life had changed in four years. I have never liked change, but God had brought healing to my life and started me on new journeys.

I do sometimes laugh at my own inadequacies and remind God that He is using a very leaky vessel to do His work. Too many folks think their vessels must be perfect before they can serve God. I had tried being perfect, but it just didn't work well. Thank God for grace. A church sign had summed it up, GRACE, GOD'S RICHES BY CHRIST'S SACRIFICE. What a glorious promise! And because of God's amazing grace, we who have lost loved ones can look forward to a grand reunion someday.

The next morning, we rode a short fifteen miles and another glorious statement on another sign also offered a promise.

WELCOME TO FLORIDA, it read. With incredible exhilaration, I rode into my final state. The beautiful promise lay just beyond the welcome message. The dreadful grooves on the shoulder ended at the Florida line, and beyond lay a three-foot, wonderfully unbroken shoulder. The thirteenth state had rolled out the welcome mat.

My cousin especially appreciated the smooth shoulder; his rightful territory had just expanded to six feet.

CHAPTER 17

Front Porches and Diners

Florida rolled out that smooth welcome mat and I was free to think of things other than avoiding shoulder grooves. The excitement of finally riding into the last state of my journey was accompanied by reflection on the incredible meetings that had already taken place.

I also had time to think about what still lay ahead. Tucked into my journal was a letter, postmarked in Florida, that had arrived at my home in Ohio shortly before I'd begun my ride. I'd brought it with me, intending to respond sometime during the weeks I was on the road. I had not yet written my reply, and now I discovered that it was possible I could deliver my response in person.

How could one book sent to a prisoner start such a chain of events? The story began when a praying mother in Florida contacted me. She was concerned about her son's spiritual condition, or, rather, the lack thereof; he claimed to be an atheist. His mother thought he might enjoy my book about hiking the Appalachian Trail.

Her son was in prison. I sent him a book and soon had a reply from him. He had enjoyed the adventure of the hike but did not believe what I had written about walking the trail in a real relationship with God. After completing the book, he had passed it on to the seventeen fellow prisoners in his cell block.

His critique of my book was well written and obviously penned with much thought and intellect. I wondered how such a brilliant mind could deny the existence of an almighty God. I tried to think like an atheist, tried to imagine myself not believing in a Creator. It was an impossible exercise for me; not believing is far more difficult than believing. How anyone can look at the composition of a flower or a tree or our bodies and deny that God exists is baffling to me.

I acknowledge, though, that while I was out riding a bicycle through dramatic canyons and majestic forests under the vast skies of God's universe, this man languished in a prison cell, steeping in anger and bitterness.

Sometime during my ride through the West, I received an email from the Mayo Correctional Institution in Mayo, Florida. I recognized the name of the institution; this was the prison where I'd sent a copy of my book. The email was not from the writer of the letter stuck in my journal, but from an instructor of GED courses for inmates at the prison.

The instructor was going through a difficult time in his life, and one of his students, an inmate serving a life term for murder, gave him the copy of *Hiking Through* that was being passed among the inmates. The student thought the messages of the book might interest his instructor.

Fourteen of the fifteen hundred inmates were enrolled in the GED class. The instructor had emailed me to ask if I would be interested in coming to the prison and speaking to the class. I sent him a reply immediately; I was on a cross-country bike ride and would get in touch with him once I was finished with the ride and had returned home.

If I consented to speak, the instructor had told me, the prison would do a background check on me before I'd be permitted inside those walls. A background check. At last, all my speeding indiscretions would be revealed.

I had never heard of Mayo and had no idea where the town was located in Florida. If the time came that I visited the prison, then I'd check a map and find the place. But I'd think about that after my ride was over.

On our last night in Georgia, I mapped our route across Florida and was amazed to discover that in two days I would be pedaling right past the Mayo Correctional Institution. I planned to take Route 27 through central Florida, and that highway ran through the little town of Mayo. What are the chances of riding coast to coast, over 4,500 miles, to find out that your route takes you past a prison that has extended an invitation to you? No, the word *coincidence* does not belong in this story.

This discovery convinced me to stop in Mayo and visit the facility. However, the background check had not yet been done, so I was quite certain I would not be permitted to pay a visit to any inmate.

"I thought Florida was flat." A voice behind me arrested my thoughts of going to prison. The road was indeed still hilly here in northern Florida. The gradual ups and downs brought us to our first town, Monticello, where beautiful old homes extended ornate front porches to welcome visitors.

We stopped at Monticello's post office for the fourth and final cleansing of my panniers. I stuffed an assortment of seats and seat covers into a box headed for home. The cheap Wal-Mart lounge chair was working beautifully; how I wished I had purchased it back in Fallon, so many miles ago. The side pockets of my panniers were beginning to bulge with my roadside booty, so several handfuls of change were also added to the box. The final addition was tucked beneath an open seam in one of the seat covers. Since I'd found that silver money clip clasping its bounty, I could no longer be nonchalant about leaving my bike unattended. That burden also went home, and my bike and my mindset were both lighter as Marv and I pedaled toward Perry, our destination that first night in Florida.

197

"How far to Mayo?" I asked the lady at the front desk.

"It's only twenty minutes down Route 27," she replied.

For what was probably the hundredth time in my ride, I asked for a translation. "How many miles is it? I'm on a bicycle; I doubt I can ride it in twenty minutes." It was amazing how few people could tell me the distance in miles between towns. Many folks had no answer for me.

We measure so many things by time. It's time to eat, it's time to sleep, and it's time to wake up. Clocks in our houses and our vehicles and on our wrists control all we do. That morning, it was time to head down the road twenty miles to the big house where they not only tell time but they do time.

Swamp land flanked both sides of Route 27. We were still a distance from the prison when we saw a large clearing in the trees and swamp. The buildings of the Mayo Correctional Institution soon appeared, set back from the highway. Fencing topped with razor wire imprisons 1,500 of society's poorly behaved members. A nondescript brick building stands guard outside the razor-fence perimeter, and just beyond that building a sign warns against unauthorized travel. Convinced I was in the "unauthorized" category, I entered the brick building and was greeted by a receptionist.

I assured the receptionist that I had no plans of moving into the neighborhood and explained my contacts in the prison and my cross-country bike ride. "And it was just so incredible that I was pedaling past this place, that I wanted to stop." That really was my only reason. I had no illusions that I might gain entrance to the world behind that fence.

"Do you wish to speak with the warden?" she asked. I stammered for a few seconds before replying, "Sure, if that's possible." This was a scenario I hadn't imagined.

After a few minutes, I was ushered into the warden's office and I explained why two bicycles were parked outside her prison. Yes, the warden was a lady. One lady in charge of 1,500 prisoners. I surmised that this was probably a lady I did not want to upset.

"You can't go inside the prison, but I will allow you to write a letter to your friend," the warden told me. "And I'll see that he gets it."

I quickly penned a letter to my godless friend. *Unless a person believes in coincidence piled upon coincidence, one would almost be convinced God brought me past your prison home*, I wrote him. *God loves you so much he brought me to your prison door to tell you that. He won't give up on you and will chase you until you either give up or run out of time.* I noted that I would be coming back to the prison to do a program after my ride was finished and I hoped to meet him then.

It was time for us to leave and it was time to eat. The Mayo Correctional Institute employs 500 people, but the town of Mayo has less than 1,000 residents. We found a small diner, the Mayo Café, catering to the local crowd. Lunch was a gustatory delight. For less than $7, I grazed the fresh fruits and desserts of the salad bar and a variety of comfort foods at the hot bar.

In the far corner of the buffet was a pan filled with mystery food. I summoned the server to inquire about the unknown vegetable.

"Those are collard greens," she replied.

"I've never tasted collard greens before. What are they like?"

"They're a leafy vegetable in the cabbage and broccoli family." I was acquainted with the cabbage family. Her comment evoked images of cabbage leaves floating from the sky. "Most folks cook them with garlic, onion, and bacon grease. We use ham bones to add flavor."

Sure enough, a large ham bone was submerged in the slimy green mixture. I enjoyed sampling the new dish; the taste of the collard greens was interesting, with just enough seasoning and pig fat to make it palatable. The experience just confirmed what I already knew from years of food service: Any food can be made tolerable with enough sugar or grease. How can a person possibly stomach a slice of rhubarb pie without obliterating most of the woeful taste with excessive sugar? I do question whether anything as indestructible as a patch of rhubarb should be eaten.

A brilliant thought occurred to me, the solution to the South's menacing creepy crawler. Kudzu salad, kudzu pie, kudzu casserole. Boil it, fry it, bake it, and dump grease and sugar on it until it's palatable. Another world problem solved.

The server had also told me that collard greens were full of vitamin K. I didn't know what vitamin K was or what it did, but I ingested plenty of it that day. My cousin had trouble keeping up with me as we left Mayo. I must have benefited from the extra vitamin K, but Marv had passed on that experience and now paid the price.

Just outside of Branford was a little settlement called Fort White. We stopped to refuel at a small store. An elderly man outside greeted everyone in sight. He sported a long white beard and wore a ball cap with a Beech-Nut logo. I commented on his cheerful demeanor.

"My name's Happy," he said with a wide grin. "I never have a bad day."

Everyone in town knew Happy, and he spent most of his day there at the store, talking with whoever stopped by.

"What do you do for a living?" I asked.

"I'm on disability. I get a check from the government every month. Folks think I'm crazy." He looked at me with that grin still in place. "I've convinced everyone I am crazy. I'm not, but I don't mind if they think that." My short conversation with him led me to believe there was a high probability that Happy might be wrong and everyone else was right, but I kept that thought to myself. Maybe a monthly check from the government is reason enough to be happy.

Happy wanted to know about my bicycle ride and I explained I was biking cross-country and had already ridden over 4,500 miles on my way to Key West. When a clerk came outside to coat her lungs with nicotine, Happy's chatter turned in her direction and he told her about my attempt at riding from one coast to another.

"Happy, I used to think you were crazy, but I know now you're not." She nodded in my direction. "But that guy, he's definitely crazy." Happy found that proclamation quite to his liking and howled with laughter.

I'd been to Florida many times before. Most folks know Florida as home to Disney World and recognize cities such as Tampa, Sarasota, Miami, and Tallahassee. Now I was traveling by bicycle and discovered towns such as Monticello, Mayo, Branford, and High Springs. In these small towns, the heart of America can be found. Homes with welcoming front porches, inviting shops, and interesting diners are the norm in such communities.

Across from our motel in High Springs was a small eatery with a retro fifties look. The Fleetwood Diner is distinguished by a large, six-foot clock on the front of the building. It's time to eat, was the message. That's always time well-spent. I had no need of more vitamin K; however, the huge plate of steaming spaghetti did supply just what my body needed to finish off another day.

We left High Springs, pedaling through an early morning mist. My eyes weren't watching the road as much as they were admiring the front porches of this small slice of America. At this early hour, the porches were empty; but I could imagine good conversations and neighborly visits and cold lemonades on these hospitable portals.

Our route ran alongside large horse farms. A low-hanging fog shrouded trees draped with moss. We pedaled silently through a dreamlike landscape.

My thoughts were also rolling through an internal landscape that felt surreal. This was our third day in Florida; this was the final state of my long journey. What I had so longed for during those lonely nights in Nevada and Utah would soon be reality. Another adventure was drawing to a close.

It's exciting to dream and chart such quests, but the end of the journey eventually comes and the dream is no longer a dream but an achievement. The endings have always been too sudden for me, too much like death itself. The dream is done. It's over.

My body was in the best shape it had seen in years. My legs kept churning out the miles. I had once again settled into a routine. And now the dream would soon be ended.

At least, I was no longer lonely. A riding companion completely changed the dynamics of my bike ride. It was good to know some-one was nearby. My bike journey had turned from a solo ride to a duo ride, and now it was going to swell into a parade.

In Sarasota, the Stoltzfus clan had been keeping tabs on my ride. Would I mind if they joined me for several days in central Florida? Marvin, Todd, Ethan, and Elliot were father, son, and grandsons. They were all experienced bikers and would be fol-lowed by an RV. The temperature in Florida was over 100, and being followed by a ready supply of cold Gatorade and an air-conditioned break room sounded great. We'd be able to escape the hot Florida sun and lounge in comfort. We agreed to have the fam-ily meet us at our motel the following morning in a place called The Villages, our destination for the night.

The Villages is a carefully planned grid of neighborhoods that declares itself to be America's most popular retirement commu-nity. With a population that's grown in the last ten years from 8,000 to 80,000 and neighborhoods that offer every activity and recreation imaginable, this place is anything but retiring. I saw a mass of humanity taking another go around at life in a place that someone tried to build and sell as the perfect world. To my eyes, it looked like one last attempt to achieve the ideal life before moving on to the next.

Walking about this fabricated world was more dangerous than bicycling Georgia's highways. The good citizens of these communities buzz everywhere on golf carts, and they whooshed by us as we explored the modern town square with its shops and restaurants. The restaurants were over-priced but busy; apparently the recession gripping the rest of the country had bypassed this community.

Early the next morning, the Stoltzfuses and the RV arrived. Introductions were made, and I became the Pied Piper of Florida. The temperature soared, and it was a joy to relax in air-conditioned comfort during our breaks. The RV was well stocked with essentials— cold beverages and chocolate snacks.

After being alone on the road for so long, I enjoyed riding with a group. It's easy to become set in our ways and to focus so exclusively on our goals that we don't allow others to take part in our journeys. On the day I took my first step on the Appalachian Trail, I had decided to be open to anyone God chose to put in my path. I carried that same decision into my bike journey across America. God chose to send me four new friends and an air-conditioned RV.

The Stoltzfuses were Florida natives and well-versed in area history. I gained insights and information about this part of Florida that I would have missed had I ridden alone.

One of the things that piqued my curiosity was the occasional tower that rose from the flat landscape. We were riding south on 27; the land was flat, most buildings two or three stories at the most. Then we would suddenly see a large, soaring edifice on the horizon. What were these towers? It turned out that there was no link between the structures, other than the fact that they all were built to tower over the landscape.

Edward W. Bok completed his 205-foot Singing Tower in 1929. Bok's story is the embodiment of what we call the American Dream. He came to the States as a child in the late 1800s and began working as an office boy in a telegraph office. His life choices made him a successful writer and publisher; he was the editor of *The Ladies Home Journal* and won a Pulitzer Prize for his autobiography. An environmentalist, he developed the Bok Tower Gardens just outside the town of Lake Wales. The tower in the botanical gardens soars to the sky and looks like a Gothic cathedral. Its bells ring out in concert twice a day.

Several miles north of Lake Wales is the town of Clermont where the Citrus Tower's observation deck overlooks the rolling landscape and acres of orange groves. This tower was built in 1956, to a height of 226 feet (about twenty-two stories), and became quite an attraction in the Orlando area for many years.

In 1961, another tower grew from the sandy loam near the town of Lake Placid. This central Florida town is known for its many murals on downtown buildings and the thousands of acres devoted to growing caladiums, an ornamental plant with broad, colorful leaves. Murals and plants are both so well known and marketed that Lake Placid has been called The Town of Murals and The Caladium Capital of the World. The 270-foot structure that overlooks the caladium fields boasts of being the world's tallest concrete block tower. It has gone through several name changes since being constructed and is now officially the Lake Placid Tower. They can call it what they wish; in reality it's still only a big pile of concrete blocks.

People and communities want to be known for something. Lake Placid boasts of the world's tallest concrete tower overlooking the world's largest caladium fields. The mindset is "Look at us. Look at what we've done." Usually the focus is on something tall or big. We have the tallest tower. We have the biggest fields. Just once, I'd like to hear someone boast about digging the deepest hole. "Come to our town and look down the deepest hole ever dug."

Riding across America, I passed through many small towns pronouncing their claim to fame. Paris, Tennessee, has the largest fish fry in the world. Murray, Kentucky, boasts that its roller-skating rink is the largest in America. Towns everywhere want to be the Capital of This or the Capital of That.

I was thinking that the towers would be more functional if they at least had a clock telling travelers when it's time to eat. My stomach, though, is persistent and reliable in its reminders. The RV had been on a scouting mission, searching for a restaurant. Now it passed us, and the grandson riding shotgun made exaggerated motions toward his wrist. His gyrations meant nothing until we pulled into the restaurant they had chosen.

"What were you trying to tell us?" I inquired.

"I was pointing to my wristwatch." Then I saw the sign at the restaurant. The name of the eatery was Clock. What a name for a restaurant. My mind clicked into restaurant-management mode and went spinning through the advertising opportunities such a name would offer. There was the obvious, "It's time to eat," and the bizarre, "Hour food served within minutes" and "You are welcome to seconds." Perhaps I need to get back into food service; all my advertising talent is going to waste.

At Lake Placid, within sight of the concrete block tower, I said good-bye to my new friends and the parade disbanded. My cousin Marv joined the other Marv and his family in their RV and returned to Sarasota. Whew! He had survived.

I would go on alone. It had been marvelous riding with a group, but it was fitting that I finish this journey just as I started it, alone.

A strange thing happens as you near the finish of a lifetime goal—the going gets extremely tough. It feels as if all heaven and earth conspire against you and say, "How badly do you want this?" I'd experienced that on my Appalachian Trail hike, and now my bike journey would turn more agonizing and frightening than anything I had yet experienced on the road across America.

CHAPTER 18

One Way

It was with mixed feelings that I pedaled out of Lake Placid the following morning. I'd grown accustomed to the companionship of my cousin on this ride, and I had enjoyed the brief time with new friends from Sarasota and the luxury of the RV. But now I was alone again. Finishing this last stretch by myself was the right thing to do, I knew, but I felt a loss when I started out that morning and there was no one in my mirror.

The tall tower of concrete blocks appeared faintly through the mist. I rode seventy-six miles to South Port, past large orange groves and sugar cane fields, watching many birds and dodging dead frogs. Gurgling springs created a waterway alongside the highway and this was home to thousands of frogs. Many had become curious about what lay outside their safe aquatic world. But forays up to the broad road had led many to destruction. Flattened frog carcasses littered the road, where each wanderer had given a final croak before falling victim to the Michelin Man. It truly had not been a good year.

Following the south shore of Lake Okeechobee from Clewiston, I arrived in South Bay at two in the afternoon. At lunch, I had stopped in Moore Haven and had more vitamin K. My body had enough energy to keep riding, but there was nothing between

South Bay and Homestead except ninety miles of swamp and sugar cane fields. I decided to go to bed early and leave before daylight the following day.

At five the next morning, I was pedaling through South Bay in darkness. At the southern edge of town I met with extreme disappointment. A grooved shoulder! Had they actually hired someone from Georgia to destroy Highway 27? The road surface was fine, but I shared that with many semi trucks also getting an early start. For the next two hours, I kept one eye on the road ahead and one eye on my mirror, watching for lights coming out of the darkness behind me. Whenever a semi appeared, I'd dodge off the road to the shoulder and tolerate a short but violent shock treatment. This course of action worked; the first shock disassembled my bones, and the second reassembled them.

Another challenge of driving in darkness is the difficulty of seeing and avoiding tire carcasses. Many truckers repair their tires with retreads. A retread tire is much like a snake in that it will shed its skin eventually. These rubber tire clumps littering the highway are a major cause of flats for bikers. Sharp steel bands in the retreads lie in wait like a silent porcupine, armed to puncture any bicycle tire.

I'd been fortunate, avoiding most of these obstacles for the last 4,800 miles; but that morning I bounced over several large unfurled retreads that I had not seen in the darkness. After each of those encounters, I spent several minutes listening intently, fearing a telltale hiss of air.

With the morning light came a wonderful sight, a sign welcoming me to Broward County. And beyond the sign, new asphalt edged with a smooth, clean shoulder stretched as far as I could see. The highway ran through open areas of swamps, saw-grass, and sugar cane fields. It was hard to imagine that just east of me were the metropolitan areas of Boca Raton, Fort Lauderdale, and Miami.

The Seminole Indians have six reservations in Florida, five of which are in the southern half. My ride had started on an Indian reservation in the opposite corner of America. Somehow, Native Americans have been pushed to the edges of our country.

Just beyond the junction where I-75 ends and becomes I-595 running to Fort Lauderdale, I stopped at a fueling station to refill my water bottle. As I rested outside, a young lady approached and inquired about my bike ride. She seemed nervous and troubled, and as we talked she told me her best friend had been her father and he had recently committed suicide.

Dear God, what do I tell her? Many folks carry whatever feelings they've had about their relationships with their earthly fathers over to their thoughts about God, the heavenly Father. This girl felt her father had abandoned her by his suicide, and she believed God had also abandoned her. I assured her that was not the case. As best as possible, I explained about a loving God who does care and wants a relationship with her. The very being of God is love, and He will never desert anyone who trusts in Him.

Ten miles later, Route 27 ended and I entered the most harrowing stretch of my entire journey thus far. Highway 997 is a narrow, two-lane highway. Not only was it extremely busy, but it had absolutely no shoulder. I was forced to merge into the stream of speeding trucks and other lesser but equally deadly vehicles. The ride was gut-wrenching and nerve-racking. Truck horns blasted and occasionally an oncoming car passed another vehicle and swerved into my lane. I came within inches of succumbing to the fate of the flattened frogs. This was indeed the valley of the shadow of death. Although I did not fear evil, I feared.

I had no time to think about anything other than the traffic, but here came another unwelcome sight. Storm clouds, dark, swirling, approaching fast. I'd been very fortunate in avoiding storms and traffic for most of my trip; now here I was, faced with the worst of both. I needed shelter and I needed it quickly.

In the distance, a huge edifice loomed against the dark sky. I could not determine what it was, perhaps a mine building, a factory, or a huge office complex. I made a mad dash for what I hoped was sanctuary.

As I drew closer, I saw the large flashing sign. This was a casino. At the intersection of Routes 41 and 997, the Miccosukee Indian casino towered over the landscape. I dashed under the large overhang at the front entrance just as the sky opened and a deluge of rain fell.

I stood outside the glass doors of that casino for one hour, waiting for the rain to abate. Gazing into the bowels of the casino, I observed hundreds of people donating money to Indian causes. It was quite amazing; the white man had taken most of the land from the Native Americans in years gone by, and now the white man was willingly paying them back. No guns, bows, and arrows were needed. Just the slight possibility of a jackpot kept folks interested in feeding the mechanical bandits in front of them.

While waiting for the downpour to end, I called my friend Ina in Ohio. She immediately detected that my spirits were lower than the bank accounts of the casino patrons inside.

"I'm so nearly done, but I've hit a wall mentally and emotionally," I complained. "This road I'm now on is terrifying."

"Just calm down, and let's pray about it," she replied. Then and there she prayed safety and protection on me. "Send him sunshine and a safe road shoulder," she implored.

Out on the highway again, I passed the intersection and the road did indeed have a shoulder; and yes, the sun did come out. It was Florida; of course the sun came out.

Although I don't believe Ina's prayer caused a road shoulder to magically appear where before there had been none, I do believe that prayer was what took me across America and brought me home again. Two evenings prior to the start of my bike journey, six of us had gathered in Ina's back yard for a prayer session. While I sat in a chair, the other five laid hands on me and each one prayed safety, peace, and God's blessing on my travels.

While you contemplate the validity of prayer, allow me to give you some facts about my journey. Almost 5,000 miles rolled under my wheels. I had one flat tire in California that I changed, none from California to Florida. With the exception of the slipped chain at the Golden Gate Bridge, the bike had absolutely no mechanical problems. I never feared theft or personal harm. I parked my bike unsecured anywhere I wished. I met incredible people and found wads of cash on the highway. I submit to you that I am either the luckiest man in the world, or all the prayers offered before and during my ride were heard and honored.

If you believe all of that was pure luck, then I missed a great opportunity at that Indian casino. I, however, know I was blessed, not lucky.

I headed for Homestead, Florida, with a new attitude and a lighter spirit. Just beyond Homestead was Florida City, my stopping point for the day. Here Route 997 intersected with Highway 1. This was the road that would take me to the Florida Keys. In two days, I'd arrive at the end of Route 1 in Key West.

From the first days of planning this journey, I had been intrigued by the fact that only one highway led to my final destination. Hundreds of highways crisscross America; I had many choices to make as I rode from Washington to Florida. But in southern Florida, Route 1 was the only road that would take me to Key West—the only route to my final goal.

That is, my friend, a picture of each person's passage through life. Throughout the journey, there are many choices to be made. But in the end, only one Way leads to the ultimate goal of life everlasting.

The next morning I rode into ten miles of major construction on Route 1. Those ten miles were the most terrifying stretch of my entire bike ride.

It was still dark when I left Florida City. I did have a bright red flashing tail light. My little headlight was not really necessary, since the lights of the cars and trucks behind me lit the way. Barriers divided an already narrow roadway, and I had no choice but to take my place in the steady stream of traffic. Horns beeped constantly, letting me know what drivers thought of having to follow a bicycle through the construction. The line of vehicles behind me grew longer every minute. Every now and then I spotted a break in the barriers and room to ride in the opposite lane. I'd jump to the other side of the barriers, riding for a short time in the wrong lane against oncoming traffic. Then approaching traffic or a narrowing of the lane would force me back between my proper boundaries.

I finally rolled free of the construction and found the safety of a good shoulder. Crossing a bridge running from the mainland to the keys, I entered Key Largo. The Florida Keys are comprised of over 100 islands and forty-two connecting bridges. The longest bridge is called the Seven Mile Bridge, I suspect because it is seven miles long. I'd been dreading that bridge ever since crossing the Astoria bridge over the Columbia River back in Oregon.

That was a bridge to be crossed tomorrow, though, and I had other worries on this day. I had been most concerned about the shoulder, or lack of it, on Highway 1. Bikers riding to Key West have told horror stories about highway conditions. I found the conditions actually better than the day before. What concerned me now was dark storm clouds approaching. I had dodged so many rainstorms. Could I avoid this one? I could see the sheet of rain coming my way.

On my left were gated oceanfront mansions. Fortunately, one gate stood open, and I saw that as my salvation. A sign attached to a post warned, PRIVATE PROPERTY, NO TRESPASSING. I was not planning to trespass; I only sought shelter. For thirty minutes, the open garage was my shelter from the passing storm. The owner never discovered the trespasser holed up in his garage. I suspect he might even have been given a few extra blessings that day, and he has no idea why.

At one o'clock, I arrived in Marathon, the last town with lodging before Key West. Another storm was rolling in, and the rain and I reached the Banana Bay Resort simultaneously. I had pedaled seventy-nine miles and was only fifty miles from Key West, but I ended my day. The rain continued all afternoon and evening, confirming my wisdom in stopping in Marathon.

At three o'clock, visitors knocked on my door. My friends from Sarasota, Ivan and Fran, were on their way to Key West to meet me at the finish line and return me to Sarasota. The last time I had seen them was in Hutchinson, Kansas, when they visited their son and his family and I had spent several days relaxing and eating Fran's cooking. They brought meat and cheese, fruits and pastries, and a variety of beverages. Among the bounty was a bottle of Coca-Cola that I intended to use in my celebration at the end of my journey. I promised to meet them in Key West the following morning about eleven o'clock.

I intended to finish the next day, even if it meant riding through fifty miles of rainstorms. As the rain pattered on the roof, I contemplated the end of this journey. I could hardly believe that I was so close to finishing my bike ride. Riding from the corner of Washington State to the far corner of Florida had sounded impossible. Yet, by getting up each day and pedaling down the road, I was about to make that impossibility a reality. I went to bed nervous and excited. And busting at the seams with all the food I had eaten.

At six in the morning, I did a weather check. Large puddles of water lay everywhere, but the rain had stopped.

I maneuvered my bicycle around the little ponds and started the final miles of my final day. By six-thirty, I was face-to-face with the Seven Mile Bridge that stretched out across the waters and disappeared into the darkness. To my relief, I had a wide shoulder. The mileage markers on Highway 1 counted down the miles to the end of the highway in Key West. Mile by mile, I pedaled across the long bridge, quietly rejoicing as my bike rolled by each mile marker.

I had started across the bridge in darkness; by the time I reached dry land, seven miles later, the morning light was glowing. My passage reminded me of the cross of Christ, another bridge from darkness to light.

Once safely across, I turned to view the bridge in daylight. In the eastern sky behind me, a large cumulus cloud billowed upward. Although it hid the rising sun, golden rays burst from all corners of the cloud. I took it as a good-morning wish from God and an encouragement to go and finish the task.

That beautiful cloud formation was behind me, but in front were those nasty dark clouds again. *Just hold off the rain for one more morning, God*, I prayed.

My ride across the country had been marked with many signs, some welcome, some disappointing, some amusing, entertaining, or admonishing. But at ten-thirty that morning, I spotted a sign that is perhaps my favorite. WELCOME TO KEY WEST...PARADISE USA.

Only two more miles. Ivan and Fran had brought their bicycles with them and now rode out to meet me. As we sailed along those final oceanfront miles, Ivan told me there was yet one more obstacle.

My goal, the end of my journey, was a buoy-shaped concrete block about ten feet tall that marks the southern corner of our country. On that day, the buoy was barricaded; it was being painted and fencing kept visitors at a distance. I had ridden 5,000 miles, and now a barricade would stop me just feet from my final goal.

We rounded a corner and the buoy came into view, with nothing but water beyond. On most days, lettering on its striped surface declares it to be at the southernmost point of the continental USA. On this day, there was no lettering. The black, yellow, and red stripes had just been given a fresh paint job. And around the buoy was a metal fence, keeping all visitors at a safe distance and bearing signs that warned of wet paint.

I coasted up to the barrier separating myself from my goal. A man stood nearby with paint brush in hand. I explained my 5,000-mile ride, my goal of reaching that final point of land, my desire to touch the buoy. And I ended with what I hoped was a polite, good-humored, yet unassailable question.

"Sir, can you think of any way you could possibly prevent me from finishing my ride at that buoy?"

I have learned you should never paint every man with the same brush. Some are kind, while some are mean and rigid. I met a painter that day who recognized the significance of the moment.

"Have your friend lift your bike over the fence, and you can squeeze around the back here. Just be careful not to touch any of the wet paint."

Ivan lifted my bicycle over the barricade. A curious crowd watched, and he announced to them that this bicycle and rider had just concluded a 5,000-mile journey across America. The crowd broke into a cheer as I opened the bottle of Coca-Cola, leaned back against the buoy, and let out a long sigh.

CHAPTER 19

It's About Time

O h, buoy, what a view! From the tip of land where I stood, I gazed down South Street and heard an echo in my spirit. Memory tugged, and I was pulled back to Dalton, Massachusetts, as Padre the priest and I strolled through town and watched families having good times together. Our conversation that day about families and front porches and finding the soul of America had been the impetus for this bicycle ride.

From the edge of our country, I now looked down a street filled with porches, simple to ornate, comfortable and welcoming. Surely no town in America can boast of more interesting front porches than Key West. Unwittingly, I had chosen to finish my journey in a place with a plethora of porches. The ride was done. I had pedaled through thirteen states, covering 4,951 miles in sixty-nine days. Another thread in my life had been taken up, spun, and woven into the larger framework of my measured time here on earth.

My ride started out as a search for what I called Front Porch America. Although my front porch experiences were limited, I did meet folks from all walks of life in many different situations. I saw the ravages of unemployment and poverty, shared with those who enjoyed an abundance of blessings, and walked the streets of retired America. I encountered people selling cans and bottles for a meager subsistence and homeless people whose respite for the night was the shelter of a bridge. I met those who still believe in hard work and helping others, and I trespassed behind the gates of privilege.

I talked with folks of many different religions and degrees of belief. I was inspired by the faith story of Bobby White and that of a new Christian whose shoes were too tight. I spoke with some whose hearts were too tight and some who had no hope of anything beyond this life. Choices and decisions, some good and some bad, had determined the path they were now walking. The saddest stories were from people who lamented bad choices and longed to go back in time and choose more wisely.

Ivan, Fran, and I also sought to go back in time; we wanted to recapture a moment we cherished. We left the buoy and pedaled down Duval Street to Ivan's parked vehicle. After loading the bikes, we went in search of a restaurant. Not just any restaurant, but the Paradise Café.

Years earlier, my wife and I had visited Key West with Ivan and Fran. Ivan and I were both in the restaurant business, and we wanted to sample local food specialties. On foot, the four of us had wandered the side streets until we found a small, out-of-the-way corner café that was noted for serving the best Cuban sandwiches in Key West. At the Paradise Café we had spent a memorable hour, having a good time and creating something of a commotion. Ivan and I, of course, watched with interest the comings and goings of a small mom and pop eatery, while the ladies were having their usual fun, laughing and talking about whatever it is that women talk about.

Now, my friends and I agreed that the Paradise Café would be the perfect place to celebrate the conclusion of my bike ride. We drove the back streets, trying to recall familiar landmarks, jubilant when at last we found the eatery.

But something was amiss. No sign designated this place as the Paradise Café; no cars were parked out front; the place had clearly shut down. We stood on the front porch and peered into the deserted interior.

The café was gone, and so was that time we had wanted to recapture. We can never go back and repeat first or wonderful events. Even if the eatery had been open, our time now would not have matched the memories we wanted to recreate. We four had had a wonderful time at the Paradise Café years ago; but sadly, it had done what many restaurants do, failed to survive. Even sadder, my wife failed to survive the disease she fought; and several years later, she passed away and left me behind. This journey through life is in one direction—forward. As badly as we would like to go back in time, we cannot.

Time is an incredible concept that seems so simple, yet scientists, theologians, and philosophers spend entire lifetimes attempting to understand exactly what time is. For all our differences in this country of ours, time is one of the few things we all have in common. Time measures, regulates, and rules our lives and gives structure to all our thinking.

Christians believe that we exist in a small amount of measured time, but that God exists forever, before and after our dimension. Believers talk about eternity and a world without time. But our thinking here in this world is saturated with the idea of time as a measurement. Even folks who deny God and His creation of the earth need to discover a beginning. They are compelled to come up with theories like the big bang, evolution, and other explanations about the birth of time, space, and mankind. For unbelievers, talking about a God who has existed forever and an eternity that never ends is foolishness.

Even for believers, the concept of forever is hard to comprehend. How can we live forever? How can a person not age? We have no way to grasp this, no way to understand, because we are so rooted in time.

I enjoy theorizing. Allow me a brief flight of speculation.

Here is a fact: Take two highly accurate atomic clocks. Synchronize them, then fly one clock around the world while the other remains stationary. The clock that has experienced movement will have lost or gained (depending on which direction you fly) a small fraction of a second. Time is altered by forward movement. Light moves at a speed of 186,000 miles per second. Is it possible that a person moving at that speed halts time and thus does not age? Is it possible that at death our souls escape our bodies at that speed and rejoin the true Light of the universe? At the end of time, when hell is cast into outer darkness, does it perhaps move at the speed of light through eternal space forever and ever?

As I pedaled along, I spent a lot of time pondering time. That dark night in Utah seemed endless (another word attempting to describe something outside time) and reminded me of the endless separation from God that a person will experience in hell. *Time, forever, eternity.* Those words looped through my mind continuously as I struggled through the long night that was the closest thing to hell I have ever experienced.

I know God has a reason for what He does in my life and a message for both myself and my readers. I'm convinced the message God gave me that night was this: *It's about time to prepare for a place where it's no longer about time.*

We drove back to Sarasota with the rain drumming against the windshield.

Rain had dampened the very first mile of my Appalachian Trail hike. Through fourteen states and more than four months, I was often caught in thunderstorms. I hated walking in rain; it would have been no surprise had I found myself sprouting mushrooms. Rain fell on me every day of the last two weeks of my hike; as I neared my final goal, I was always cold and miserably wet.

Perhaps that was one of the reasons I pedaled like a madman to outrun any storm clouds that appeared as I biked across America. I had been fortunate, avoiding most rain storms that might have soaked me. In southern Florida, I dodged afternoon showers, imploring God to allow me to stay dry yet one more day.

As we left Key West, the rain started. It continued all afternoon and evening. It was as if God had held back the rain for one solitary bike rider but was now allowing it to fall freely once again.

On January 4, 2011, a news flash came over the Associated Press wires. Sometime over the weekend, vandals in Nevada had cut down a 70-foot cottonwood known as the Shoe Tree. The cottonwood was filled with hundreds of pairs of shoes tossed there by passing motorists. The owner of nearby Old Middlegate Station scheduled a memorial for the tree on February 13. One news site described the attack on the tree as having been committed by "dastardly vandals." The few residents of Old Middlegate Station were shocked and angered at the destruction of the famous tree.

I remembered the vivid colors of the evening when I biked to that same tree. The sun was setting, and brilliant red and gold rays emanated from behind the distant mountains. The tree was a wonder; shoes hung from every branch and thousands of pairs lay heaped around the base of the tree. How many years had folks been throwing up their sacrifices of footwear, observing this ritual of the Shoe Tree?

I thought about all the characters I'd met at Old Middlegate Station and reflected on the unlikely friendship that had sprung up between liberal Cynthia McKinney and this conservative Holmes County Mennonite. Our paths crossed that first evening as I walked across the gravel parking lot; we stood outside and got acquainted as darkness settled in. Our differences of opinion on almost everything were immediately apparent; yet our conversation that evening was sacred.

"Cynthia, there is so much hate in Washington. Someone needs to start a dialogue where love and respect is the foundation," I said.

"Hate sells," was her reply.

"Hate may sell for a while, but love will triumph in the end. Cynthia, you may be the person who can redirect the bitter conversations taking place in our nation's capital."

"We're being interviewed by the news media when we arrive in D.C. You're welcome to join us." But I had my own schedule to adhere to and declined her invitation to meet at the Capitol.

Weeks after my ride was over, I saw a news article about Cynthia McKinney. The article mentioned that she had ridden across America with a group on bicycles. In the interview, Cynthia spoke about her experiences on her ride. "There is so much hatred in this town," she was quoted. "We need to start a conversation based on love."

I was amazed and humbled. God had directed me to that desert parking lot to fulfill an appointment He had scheduled.

One January day while trying to write this tome and confronted with yet another mental block, I abandoned my keyboard and visited a graveyard. Over forty-four years had passed since I'd last stood by my friend's grave. When Ivan was buried, his church had just been built and he was the first person planted in the new garden of rest. As I walked toward the church, I recalled that cemetery, with one fresh, solitary grave.

Rounding the corner of the church, I was surprised by thirty additional plantings in this sacred place. The garden lay quiet, waiting. Someday, when directed by the keeper of all such gardens, this silent spot will burst into life.

I walked among many memories that day, recognizing most of the names. The lives represented by those headstones had woven threads into the fabric of my own life, some with only a small touch, others playing a much greater role. Everyone we meet adds something to our stories, as we do to theirs.

None in that graveyard, however, had as great an impact on my life as my fourteen-year-old biking partner. Long I stood in silence, remembering that fateful night. Now Ivan was in his forty-fifth year of his first day in Heaven.

An email arrived in January. Would I be willing to come to the Mayo Correctional Institution in Mayo, Florida, to give a program to the fourteen students receiving their GED degree? The prison has a voluntary program for prisoners wanting to further their education, and the school instructor had sent the email. This was an invitation I couldn't refuse.

On my drive from Ohio to Florida, I recalled the day I had pedaled my bicycle up to the prison gates and faced those walls covered with razor wire. What was it like behind those walls? I was about to find out.

The instructor met me and we cleared security. (Apparently my speeding tickets had not been too grave a blot on my record.) Seated in the chaplain's office, we went over the program for the graduation ceremony. I had built my presentation around the things that the Appalachian Trail hike had taught me about life. Fourteen students were graduating, but I was told that other prisoners would also be attending. My book had been making the rounds among the inmates; many had either read or heard about my hike and preferred listening to me rather than sitting in their jail cell.

Almost one hundred inmates crowded the chapel. My nervous system took emergency measures and my heartbeat quickened as I faced this gathering of humanity, representing many races and religions. Murderers, thieves, and rapists sat waiting for my words. I've spoken to many groups, but this was by far the most unique group of men yet. It was also the most captive audience I've had. *God, give me the right words*, I prayed.

Whenever I'm confronted with stressful situations, I resort to my own brand of humor. Laughter just has a way of releasing pressure and stress. I thanked the men for inviting me into their gated community. It seemed like a decent place to live; security was good. Whew! They enjoyed the humor.

Speaking to these men was one of the most humbling opportunities I've been given. I compared the heavy pack I carried on the Appalachian Trail to the burden of sin and guilt we carry. I compared the sign at the summit of Mt. Katahdin to the cross where I dropped my heavy burden. "With Jesus in your heart," I told them, "you can be totally free behind these prison walls. Many folks are going about their lives outside prison walls, but are locked up in their own cells of unbelief."

Following the graduation ceremony, I also spoke to a group of men attending classes preparing them for release from prison and reentry into society. Later, I asked the prison chaplain in charge of that class if he could detect which prisoners would be likely to reoffend and return to prison.

"I certainly can," he replied.

"What's the key? What is the common characteristic in prisoners that causes them to go back to old ways?" His answer surprised me.

"Pride," he said. "A person filled with pride believes he can do anything he wants to do and get away with it. He thinks he's at the top of the food chain and does not have to answer to anyone."

That is a characteristic of many prisoners, including those who walk freely in society. Many are captives of their pride. Satan had Heaven, until he gave in to his pride. That evil, the mindset of "I am, I will," can imprison us quickly and completely if we are not on guard against it.

Unfortunately, I never met the inmate to whom I'd first sent my book, the man who had written a critique of my story and claimed to not believe in God. At the time of my visit, he was in solitary confinement for an infraction and was not permitted to attend. I found it interesting that a person who denies God had been so greatly used by God. Either you believe in coincidence after coincidence, or you believe God loves that young man so much that He won't give up on him. God will either continue to send agitators like me to prick his pride, or his stubborn pride will doom him. His soul is in the balance, and a decision waits.

That young man's decision is really not much different than the decision confronting all of us. What time is it in your life? Is it time to make some changes? It is probably later than you think; but if you're reading this, there is just enough time to finish right.

On my flight back to Ohio after my ride was finished, I glanced out the window and noticed thousands of tiny white clouds beneath the aircraft. A veritable cotton field floated in the sky. I thought about the cotton fields of Alabama, the flat plains of Kansas, the moist forests of Oregon. Now I watched the panorama unfold below as, in only minutes, we flew over some of the countryside through which I had so laboriously pedaled a week ago.

A vantage point of 25,000 feet in altitude gave me a new perspective on the landscape I had previously observed from a bicycle seat. Distance will do that. At times, we do well to step back, review where we have been, and consider the direction in which we're headed.

Over four years had passed since my wife had moved to a new life. Then, I was gripped by the grief of my loss, and nothing made sense. Now, looking back over the past four years, I see a picture starting to come into focus. It's clear to me that God called Mary home precisely on time. God had both a message for me and a message He wanted me to pass on to you. The message of hope is that God is in control and is returning soon to take His children home. And God also wants folks to prepare for an unending life hereafter.

God dislodged me from my comfortable existence at home and work so that I would pay attention to these messages and deliver them to anyone who will listen. My subsequent hiking and biking—what might look like simply walking and pedaling—were actually huge jumps, leaps of faith into unknown and unmarked territory. The decisions to set forth on these journeys were more difficult than you might imagine. Remember, I like routine and safety. But my choice to believe what God says has led me down a path of incredible adventures.

My hope is that you will also choose this narrow way that will lead you to an eternal home. Someday the summons will be made for you, too. I am often reminded of my mother's call at dusk. No matter where my feet had roamed that day, her call from our front porch reached me. "Come home. It's suppertime."

I await that call from Jesus. "Come home, son. It's time!" How exciting that will be to reunite with loved ones who have gone before us, to have all our tears wiped away, and to know we will never again have to say good-bye or farewell.

Forever will have begun.

ACKNOWLEDGMENTS

Thanks to all the wonderful folks I met on my journey across America. I never imagined the amazing encounters I would have as I crossed this great country of ours. The heart of America is not in our capitol buildings, in our headlines, or in Hollywood. It's in the friendly neighborhoods, diners, factories, truck stops, churches, ice cream spots, small businesses, and farms all across our land.

Thanks to Ivan and Fran Miller for their friendship through years of restaurant management and during Mary's illness and death. Thanks also for hauling me around the Kansas landscape and picking me up in Key West, Florida.

Thank you also to my cousin Marvin Miller for joining me on my ride and for a lifetime of memories.

Thank you to my editor, Elaine Starner, for again assisting me with this project. Elaine understood this was more than just a bicycle ride, and she knows the importance of the message God gave me. Some of my darker humor was rendered a lighter shade due to her intuitions. I was probably spared some deserved criticism, but that's why it's good to be surrounded by smart and trustworthy people.

Finally, thank you to you, my readers, for your support and words of encouragement. If not for your interest and purchase of my work, I would need to find an actual job.

Folks have asked what my next project will be. All sorts of interesting suggestions have been made. I will await God's leading. In the meantime, I've started work on a book of fiction tentatively entitled *The Wanderers*. It is about two…well, I think I'll just let you wonder.

I leave you with some timely words from a wise king and a few words from a wise guy. King Solomon taught that there was a time for everything. A time to be born and a time to die, a time to plant and a time to harvest, a time to weep and a time to laugh, a time to mourn and a time to dance, a time to search and a time to give up, a time to be silent and a time to speak, a time to love and a time to hate, a time for war and a time for peace.

There is also a time to write and a time to stop writing, a time to read and a time to stop reading.